Turning the Gorgon

A Meditation on Shame

Sandra Edelman

Spring Publications, Inc.
Woodstock, Connecticut

Published by Spring Publications, Inc., 299 East Quassett Road, Woodstock, CT 06281, e-mail: spring@neca.com. Text printed on acid-free paper in Quebec, Canada. First printing 1998. Cover and text design by Brian O'Kelley.

Table of Contents

With deepest gratitude

to

Puanani Harvey

What I am trying to
say is hard to tell and
hard to understand
. . . unless, unless, you
have been yourself at
the edge of the Deep
Canyon and have
come back unharmed.
Maybe it all depends
on something within
yourself . . . whether
you go out to meet
death or to Seek Life.

—A Tewa elder
from San Juan Pueblo, New Mexico
(From Laski, *Seeking Life*)

Foreword

I should say at the outset that in some ways this book is a rogue. To be frank, there were times during its writing when what I was saying, put up against received psychological theory, seemed almost preposterous. To remind myself that it was not, I had to keep coming back to the only tether I had: the reality of my own experience. But even when I did that, the old critical voice would ask how I could possibly think that my experience would have relevance for anyone else—how could I dare argue from a particular to anything approaching a universal? In other words, there were times when working on this book was itself a source of shame.

Two answers were finally able to quell the question. One is that since I am not an entirely unique individual, some of what can be understood and said of me can be understood and said of others—a belief supported by what others have told me of their own experiences with shame. The other answer is that two signal approaches to the psyche, the Freudian and the Jungian, began with individuals working to understand their own psyches. Not that this text attempts a new metapsychology, a task for which I am prepared neither by clinical experience nor by inclination. I hope and believe that it does offer a new way of understanding and responding to shame.

The book is a "rogue" in that it deviates from the usual practice of addressing either the practitioner or the layperson. Rather, it hopes to address both more or less simultaneously. For that reason, it mingles the personal with the clinical and the scholarly, since my hope is to allow the shame-carrying lay reader to see a process which may lead to deeper understanding, but also to suggest to practitioners that there is sometimes an overlooked existential layer at the root of shame. Accordingly, I have grounded the text in observations made by clinicians as well as by authors working in disciplines other than psychology.

This duality is not a deviation from my own experience in analysis but a retracing of it, since my personal process moved along through activity of the intellect as well as through the more important "activities" of dreams, affects, and regressions. I want to emphasize, however, that the experience of the inner configurations came first, with its own unorganized knowledge. Perhaps *knowing* would be a more apt word here: unorganized knowing. Reading became part of the work to illuminate, amplify, and organize, to convert the knowing into knowledge, to *understand* what I *knew*. I did not begin with a theoretical construct and search through the literature trying to find support for it.

The structure of the book, then, stays fairly close to the pattern of my exploration, which started in the narrow sense on the day when the disturbing affects I had for years ascribed variously to the Negative Animus or Negative Mother or panic attacks or Wounded Child complex were identified by my analyst as affects of shame and fear flooding up from the infantile psyche. (I hasten to add that this is my summation; the analyst's words were gentler, neither so clinical nor so bald.) I had already had thirteen years or so of analysis by then, so I felt a bit like the actor who after a decade of theatre work is "discovered overnight"—my neurosis found sitting like Lana Turner at the counter of Schwab's drugstore.

During the week following that session, I read somewhere that the Greeks had a goddess of shame, Aidos, and that she was said to have been the young Athene's nursemaid. Later, my analyst reminded me of the Athene-Medousa myth and the ambiguities of Athene's parentage. These were all I needed to set me off on what turned out to be a year-long study essentially aimed in the beginning at finding out what it could possibly mean for a glorious figure such as Athene to have been nursed and tended by Shame. From this, I hoped to discover some instruction about how we might deal today with our shame issues. The results of that investigation make up the second chapter and its appendix.

We travel to Greece with good reason for reflection on and comparison to the concerns of our lives. Among those reasons is that the collective psyche which produced Greek myth is in structure no different from that of the modern Western psyche, and those myths can reveal something of our selves. Living in a Western culture, our psyches have been informed by the old Hellenic myths and philosophies which make up a significant part of our heritage. Writes James Hillman, the "emotion-charged image of Greece . . . has maintained its charge of emotion by means of *a continuing body of myths* . . . persisting in consciousness from post-Hellenic times until today" (Hillman 1975, 29). Philosopher Paul Ricoeur notes that "our philosophy is Greek by birth" and that "the originally Greek question," what is being?, belongs "inescapably to the structure of our cultural memory. . . . More precisely, the *encounter* of the Jewish source with the Greek origin is the fundamental intersection that founds our culture" (Ricoeur 1967, 20). And Max Zeller, exploring psychological interpretations of myth, says of the Greek myths, "As his great contribution, C. G. Jung recognized that the same image-creating forces are still at work today, within ourselves, in our own psyche. In fact they make our lives. . . . We encounter them as benevolent or demonic, as the source of bliss and curse, and, last but not least, they are present in every creative act. In short, they belong to our innermost nature, they are the essence of our very being" (Zeller 1990, 59).

But a shared *mythos* is not our only reason for exploring the meaning of the Greek archetypes. We also have shared cultural dominants. Consider these qualities: "energy, enterprise, daring, ingenuity, originality, and curiosity; but also restless instability, discontent with one's lot, persistent and pointless busyness, meddling interference, and mischievous love of novelty." The United States? No, Classical Athens as described by William Arrowsmith in defining the concept of *polupragmosune*, a "concept which Athenians used as a general description of their most salient national characteristics" (Arrowsmith 1969, 3).

In both cultures we find a high degree of extraversion. In Greece this so obtained that no less a mind than Aristotle's was led to conclude that "The man who is incapable of working in common, or who in his self-sufficiency has no need of others, is no part of the community, like a beast, or a god" (*Politics*, 1253a.4, Jowett trans.).

Arguably a correlative of extraversion, at least in its extreme and unconscious form, is intense concern with collective judgements about and/or against the individual, a concern which predominated in Greek culture and tends to predominate in ours. Perhaps a concomitant of this concern is the spotlight on the hero-celebrity, in both cultures associated with valuation of youth, physical beauty, prowess on the sports/battlefield, wealth, and membership in an aristocracy or upper class.

Both cultures are patriarchal, that is, are systems based on male privilege and power. Both are highly competitive, esteeming worldly fame and success. And finally, both are "shame cultures" in the sense of the classifications first made by anthropologist Ruth Benedict (1946): we rely on external sanctions to define and effect acceptable behavior, and shame results less from behavior *per se* than from being exposed—caught in behavior unacceptable to the collective. Further discussion on this point is included in the first chapter, which provides an overview of clinical perspectives on shame.

I was not allowed for long to stay in the intriguing but too comfortable intellectual pursuit of Athene and her historical background. Dreams and the process of analysis pulled me out of the heady air of scholarship back into the *humus* where the real work goes on. Perhaps Athene, originally connected with "tilth," as classical scholar Jane Ellen Harrison remarks—with the hard work of farming, with harvest, with guardianship of the family food supply—was watching over my process. But I did not dream of Athene. Instead, the unconscious presented me with this:

Seated at an outside table on a college campus, I am being shown photographs of a serial killer I have volunteered to find, the police having failed in their attempts. A woman is leafing through the photographs with me. She suddenly stops and whispers, alarm in her voice, "He is up there watching you!"

I turn and look up, to my left, to see him standing on a terrace above us, stock still, partially hidden by bushes and vines. He does not move when I look at him; he wants me to know he is there and that he has seen me. I cannot tell whether it is my knowing that he is a serial killer or the laserlike intensity of his long gaze which is menacing.

He is in his fifties, wearing a black tanktop which reveals his muscular build. Jeans complete his dress. His head is totally bald and although because of our relative spatial positions I would not in diurnal reality be able to see the top of his head, I see that a large blue-gray tattoo is there, a strange runic or glyphic pattern.

B. (a woman who works in public relations) comes by and says to me, "I wouldn't want to be in your shoes right now!" I don't need to ask what she means. I am increasingly apprehensive but unswerved. My alarm is more a recognition of reality that the task will not be as safe as it might have been had he not seen me, and I will have to be more cautious, more aware, more self-protective. But there is no question of reneging.

In a tribal society this would be acknowledged as a "big dream," and I certainly received it as such. Recognizing that it may never be fully amplified or understood, the analyst and I lived in and around it for several weeks. From that work emerged these most salient results:

— The glyphic symbol clearly operates in the religious dimension. At first it seemed to me that the figure, whom I soon gave the name Hannibal Lecter (from *Silence of the Lambs*), in large part because of his uncanny intelligence, was in some ineffable way connected to the Divine. What is even more ineffable is that I came to understand him as my internalized god image.

— This recognition inevitably led to what is still, in our culture, a daring contemplation of the reality of the dark side of the divine, what Rudolf Otto calls "the daemonic sacred." After spending some time in this contemplation, I knew that this was the energy field into which my deepest shame experiences had plunged me—the dark place I had described to my analyst as the unspeakable existential Void, where I would be at once threatened with annihilation and eternally kept conscious so that the torment would go on and on, without hope of release or cessation. Eventually, analysis enabled me to understand that this is an experience taking place in the earliest, infantile layer of the psyche, one which lies at the juncture of the personal unconscious and the collective unconscious. Or perhaps it would be more accurate to say at the juncture where the personal unconscious is just beginning to develop "above" the collective unconscious.

— The unrelenting gaze of the Hannibal Lecter figure is extremely meaningful to me, having spent much of my life feeling essentially "unseen," a feeling I can now trace to infancy and childhood and failures of maternal empathy, and a feeling which reached such depths in me that I often felt unseen by the Transcendent as well. In one of those mysterious passages of grace, the gaze came to lose its menace (I had asked in my journal, "With being seen comes the risk of being devoured?") and became a source of deep joy: I felt not only seen but acknowledged and loved, if in a stern, unsentimental way, and came to feel love in return for this commanding figure who might so easily have been seen only as a hideous threat. I felt what Ann Belford Ulanov describes as "the presence of an other, a non-ego, a subject objectively there that takes our own ego as the object of its attention and care." (Ulanov 1987, 30)

My gratitude for this "passage of grace" is boundlessly increased by the knowledge that the Lecter figure, as well as the "dark place," could have been experienced in a severely disintegrative way—could have led to a profound pathology. I have to wonder whether the seeds of transformation and the seeds of psychosis come from the same source. Perhaps they do, or perhaps it is only that change always necessarily entails some degree of disintegration, or de-integration, and that it is the flexible strength of the ego which is the crucial factor in determining whether "falling apart" leads to positive or negative transformation.

A good deal more could be said about this dream and its amplification, but my purpose here is to share the personal experience which led to the third chapter, where I discuss some of the material which sheds light on that experience. To that discussion are added the conclusions I was able to draw. Without the dream, I would not have had the audacity, perhaps not the imagination, and emphatically not the certitude, required to venture into that territory.

Three more reasons why this book is a bit of a rogue. While it is fundamentally grounded in Jungian psychology—the foundation of my personal analysis to which, if it is not too melodramatic to say so, I owe much of my life—it is not exclusively "Jungian." The insights of clinicians working from other perspectives, notably those of the object relations and Kohutian, have been extremely helpful. In fact, it seems possible that all schools of psychological thought are unwittingly working towards the psychological equivalent of what in physics is known as the unified field theory.

"Meditation" may seem a misnomer for the structure and nature of the text. I use the word not in its Eastern or New Age sense, but with a connotation which relates it to its root meaning, "taking the measure of." Forced to study my own issue, I try to take the measure of shame, its dimensions in cultural, clinical, and personal perspective.

Finally, the book does not offer a neat formula for "healing"; no list here of ten things to be done daily to rid the psyche of shame. To shed ourselves of shame we would have to shed our histories, our parentage, our personalities as they now are, and start from the beginning again. Attractive as that prospect may seem at times, despite its patent impossibility, it is implicit with unwillingness to embrace our unique life and our special destiny. To use a Christian metaphor, it is Jesus refusing to be crucified, or Jesus refusing to be Christ. And even if it were possible, to lose a sense of shame is to risk being shameless, to fly to the other polarity where decency, justice, fairness, the capacity for awe, all the elements which make up an ethical life, are obliterated. There we would lose the capacity for humility, our groundedness in our status as human. It is instructive to let the imagination play with the related etymologies: the little language cluster which gives us "humility" also gives us *humus*, earth, and *homo*, human being (both from the Latin); the Greek *khthon*, earth, thus our "chthonic," and *khamai*, "on the ground," from which we derive several nouns, including "chameleon"; in the old Germanic, the word for "earthling," and in Old English *guma*, which denotes both "man" and "bridegroom." All these suggest that to lose a sense of shame is to lose the capacity for humility and to risk becoming inflated, of being puffed up with the more-than-human. And this happens to be the root meaning of our word "evil": the exceeding of the proper limit.

On the other hand, if for us the affect of shame has become a pervasive, chronic, and radical overshadowing of our innermost self, then of course we want and need to find a way both to understand that condition and to change it, to gain a heightened sense of well-being. For virtually all of us, being "healed" in the sense of cure, of being rid of the condition, is out of the question because the past cannot be brought into the present and made to be different from what it is, was, and shall always be. But we can surround the condition with a strengthened ego position, enabling a broader perspective, more compassion for self, and

freer access to creativity and to life. These possibilities are the meditation of the final chapter.

Years before I knew very much about Jung or his view of the psyche and
before I had entered analysis, I had a mysterious, unforgettable experience during my first trip to Greece. On a spring morning at
Mycenae—which in 1969 still worked its magic, still held a sense of
vigorous life almost 3,000 years after its demise—I sat to rest on one of
the vestigial walls. The Argive plain, reaching out to the bay at Nauplion,
was mantled in a pale amber haze and the only sound I could hear was
the muffled clatter of hooves, the wild goats clambering over the nearby
cliffs. Leaning back, braced by one arm, my hand in the cool young
grasses, I fell into a reverie. Some minutes later, I became aware that the
back of my hand was being touched; the sensation was nearly imper-
ceptible, delicate as a whisper. Looking down, I discovered a tiny, most
elegant snake, no more than six inches long, her back an almost incan-
descent emerald green, her belly golden. We looked at each other for
what seemed a very long time, the snake and I, she with her brilliant
black eye not much larger than a poppy seed, her little pink tongue
flicking now and then as though she would speak. We gazed together
and then she slowly continued her way into the grass, moving with a
grace nearly too grand for so small a creature.

I did not know then about the Snake goddess or about Athene's origins
and her associations with snakes, but I knew beyond a doubt that I had
received a visitation, one which had something of royalty about it. The
word "numinous" was not in my vocabulary in those days, but my instinctive, intuitive self knew that something important had happened, for I had
been held in a moment of awe, and after the snake had gone I found myself
catching my breath.

The memory of that time has come back to me often in the working of
this material, and the thought has crossed my mind that perhaps Athene
was calling me to it even then, more than two decades ago in that high
citadel which was her first home on the Argive.

Chapter One

An Overview of Shame

To be accursed without being cursed by anybody is the highest degree of accursedness, as Kafka shows. . . . To become oneself the tribunal of oneself is to be alienated.

— Paul Ricoeur in *The Symbolism of Evil*

The experience of shame is so common in human life as to argue for its presence in the psyche as a structural given. It can be located in virtually every culture, in any era. Although the circumstances likely to precipitate shame are diverse, since diverse cultures produce diverse norms, phenomenologically the experience of shame and its outer manifestations are pretty much the same the world over: blushing, lowering of the eyes or other avoidance of eye contact, lowering of the head so that the face cannot be seen. Subjective descriptions of the experience also indicate that the inward effects are substantially the same: we feel that the ground is opening up and that we will disappear into the abyss (or we wish to); there is a desire for flight away from the source of shame, accompanied by a feeling of paralysis, as though we were unable to move at all; our mental acuity diminishes, leaving us with a feeling that where there used to be a working mind there is now a slow-moving ooze—paralysis of the intellect; we sometimes have the sensation of intense heat from what I have called the "existential blush," which registers in some strange place which is not just psyche and not just soma but both at once, as though a hellish flame had located the precise juncture of bodyself and soulself, the infinitesimal stem from which our life sprung. These are, of course, among the extreme manifestations of shame. It can also occur as a milder affect, producing a slight blush, a temporary stammer, a fleeting loss of confidence.

That shame is so common comes as no surprise, if for no other reason than that we live in what anthropologists have called a "shame culture," in contradistinction to a guilt culture. We do so for the most part unknowingly, covertly, for we like to believe that we live instead in a guilt culture, often held to be a sophisticated advance over the more "primitive" form of social control. We like to think that we live in a society in which, in the words of W. H. Auden, "the conscience of the adult individual has become internalized so that his judgement of his thoughts and actions is independent of the approval or disapproval of others and even of whether or not others are aware of them. His answer to the question 'Who am I?' is given, not in terms of his past history but in terms of what he believes and loves . . . " (Auden 1958, 8)—a guilt culture. Certainly there are individuals who have reached this point, but the prevailing tenor of American society in particular is that of a shame culture, in which "social approval is the only standard by which . . . to distinguish right action" and the "question 'Who am I?' is answered in terms of past fact—'I am the child of such and such a family and I have done this or that,'" in which "A person's own conception of who he is and the conception of others are, therefore, identical" (ibid., 5-7). In such a society, performance and conformity to prevailing standards are all. An act is not wrong unless one is caught in it; *perceptions* of one's worth *create* one's worth, which need not originate either in reality or in one's inner stature: the esteem in which one is held is the chief parent of one's self-esteem. In such a society, if aging is shameful, face-lifts and cosmetics are the antidote; if poverty is shameful, an Armani suit, even if obtained through theft as long as the theft goes undetected, provides the solution. Personal transgression kept out of the newspapers is as good as obliterated from memory, made not to have happened. In such a society overt behavior and appearance become the *sine qua non* by which we are judged as acceptable or not, and behavior and appearance then become the dominant areas of experience most vulnerable to shaping and control by the act of shaming. Thus, for most of us, from toilet training through the nursing home, the messages we have heard have not been validations of the authentic self but directives to conform to an outer image consonant with existing norms—norms which may or may not coincide with the basic patterns of the original self.

Despite such a social matrix and the prevalence of shame in individual lives, despite the fact that shame is perhaps the most painful and destructive affect of all affects, it has received, until recently, scant attention from psychologists. This lack of attention is generally noted by the handful of professionals who have written on the subject. In that literature, we often find the comment that it is as though the very existence of shame is in itself a source of shame. There even seems to be a semantic problem with the whole issue, since psychologists—at least those who have ventured into print—seem still to be groping towards a definitive etiology and taxonomy of shame as well as towards a differentiation between shame and guilt. It is almost as though the affect is so overwhelming, even to the most distanced and trained mind, that language itself cannot break it down into mutually exclusive aspects; it's as though we were trying to cut a mercury globule into neat slices.

Having said this, however, I believe it will be helpful to take a brief look at some of what has been written about shame. My purpose here is twofold: to provide an overview for the reader who many not have worked through the major literature on the subject; and to establish background for the present effort, in part to be able to depart from it with what I hope will be a meaningful addition to our understanding of shame.

Jung, writes Peer Hultberg, "rarely uses the concept of shame, and it occurs almost only in his early works. . . . [It] plays hardly any part in Jung's later work" (1988, 111). However, Mara Sidoli infers implications involving shame from Jung's *Aion*, where, she writes, he "linked feelings of shame caused by the experience of one's own inadequacy and the shadow archetype" (1988, 131). Her reference may be to the following passage in that work:

> The shadow is a moral problem that challenges the whole ego-personality, for no one can become conscious of the shadow without considerable moral effort. To become conscious of it involves recognizing the dark aspects of the personality as present and real. . . . Affects occur usually where adaptation is weakest, and at the same time they reveal the reason for its weakness, namely a certain degree of inferiority

and the existence of a lower level of personality. On this lower level with its uncontrolled or scarcely controlled emotions one behaves more or less like a primitive, who is not only the passive victim of his affects but also singularly incapable of moral judgment. (Jung 1959, 8-9)

Erich Neumann (1990) observed that a disturbed primal relationship— i.e., one in which the mother cannot or does not provide a holding environment for the infant—produces in the infant the primary feeling of guilt, a central symptom of the disturbed relationship and "characteristic of the psychic disorders of Western man." Neumann's way of understanding the infant's dynamic is, perhaps surprisingly, rather Kleinian:

> The need to counteract the lack of love resulting from the disturbed primal relationship causes the child not to blame the world and man, but to feel guilty. This type of guilt feeling appears in an early [pre-ego] phase and is archaic. . . . [It] is not a matter of conscious reflection in the child, but it leads to the conviction, which will play a determining role in the child's existence and development, that not-to-be loved is identical with being abnormal, sick, "leprous," and above all "condemned." (Neumann 1990, 86)

As we shall soon see, this is the vocabulary not of guilt but of shame, and I believe that Neumann, were he alive to complete and revise this work (he died before completing the first draft), would make that change.

Edward Edinger's "alienation neurosis," which results from the break in the ego-Self relationship caused by early parental rejection, may also be understood in terms of primal, ontic shame.

> An individual with such a neurosis is very dubious about his right to exist. He has a profound sense of unworthiness with all the symptoms that we commonly refer to as an inferiority complex. He assumes unconsciously and automatically that whatever comes out of himself—his inmost desires, needs and interests—must be wrong or somehow unacceptable. (Edinger 1974, 56)

Parental rejection stemming from the projection of the parent's shadow onto the child, he writes, is:

an unconscious process experienced by the child as something inhuman, total, and irrevocable. It seems to come from an implacable deity. This appearance has two origins. In the first place the child's projection of the Self on to the parent will give that parent's actions a transpersonal importance. Secondly, the rejecting parent who is functioning unconsciously will be acting in his own area of ego-Self identity and will therefore be inflated in an identification with deity. The consequence from the child's standpoint is a damage to his ego-self axis that may cripple his psyche permanently. (Ibid., 39-40)

Sidoli found in her own work with analysands that shame always takes place in a social context and that

for shame to be experienced it seems necessary for a baby to have developed an ego sufficient to be able to acknowledge himself and his mother and other people in the environment as separate and endowed with certain good or bad attributes. This . . . is usually established towards the end of the first year of life, reaching its peak in the various phases of toilet training and during the Oedipal stage [when] jealousy and rivalry of the parent of the same sex are at their highest and are accompanied by feelings of shame at one's own inadequacy. (Sidoli 1988, 131)

Hultberg believes that shame results from the violation of certain ideal norms and is connected with a fear of exclusion from human society, or abandonment. "It is not a fear of physical death, but of psychic extinction," he writes, having cited a passage from John Keats which he amplifies with this moving and, in my experience, accurate commentary:

The thought that hell might be a state of eternal shame, shame that is overwhelming and all-consuming pain, encompassing both body and soul, implying utter physical destruction while yet one is being kept intensively alive and conscious—this thought seems to me to express best man's awareness of the deeply distressing experience of shame. (Hultberg 1988, 115)

Based on introjected figures who "turn ominous" when the ego no longer matches their demands and who therefore threaten "abandonment, expulsion, or emotional starvation," shame may become so profound that the "psyche is threatened by disintegration." This, Hultberg writes, "is the almost indescribable fear which manifests itself as a feeling that the earth will open up and swallow the individual. . . . It is the fear of psychic death which is felt as an equivalent to extinction—destruction of the personality without any possibility of resurrection" (Ibid., 116).

We leave the Jungians and move to Freud, who, according to Andrew Morrison (1989, 47), viewed shame "as an intrapsychic reaction formation against the voyeuristic drive and as a response to the experience of being scrutinized publicly in naked vulnerability." Similarly, Gershen Kaufman, in his own overview of the literature, says that Freud relates the origins of shame to genital deficiency (1989, 8), and Sidoli that for Freud "prohibitions against exhibitionism drive the ego to create a shame feeling that obliterates awareness of the forbidden wishes" (1988, 131). According to Hultberg (1988, 111), Freud almost never referred to the concept of shame except in *The Interpretation of Dreams*, where it is mentioned in connection with embarrassment in dreams about being naked. "Apart from this he uses it almost exclusively in connection with disgust and considers shame and guilt as an express [sic] of . . . defence . . . against the drives, especially the sexual drive. Later he added the concept of morality, so that after 1910 he works with a triad of resistance or defence phenomena, as we would call them today—shame, disgust, morality."

The assertion of Piers and Singer that shame originates in the failure to live up to one's ego ideals and that the underlying fear is the fear of contempt (1953) is taken up by Helen M. Lynd (1958), who holds that shame is based on outside disapproval, is a wound to self-esteem, "a painful feeling or sense of degradation excited by the consciousness of having done something unworthy of one's previous idea of one's own excellence" and also a "peculiarly painful feeling of being in a situation that incurs the scorn or contempt of others" (ibid., 23). Always connected in some way with exposure of one's vulnerable aspects, either to others or to one's own eyes, shame is caused by a discrepancy between the ego ideal and the exposed truth; this discrepancy causes one to lose a sense of self-identity.

For Léon Wurmser (1995), writing from an object relations perspective, shame can be classified either as "realistic"—stemming from

24

an event in outer reality—or "internalized," which is the more archaic of the two forms. Later, he refers to internalized shame as basic, or radical, shame, whose root, he believes, is "the pain of essential unlovability." Such pain

is beyond speech. Ibsen called it the crime of "soul murder"—this bringing about of unlovability. . . . How much inner work is done to avert this! How much horror dwells in this hellish profundity of ultimate unlovability—as man, as woman, as child! . . . The basic flaw for which one is ultimately ashamed is therefore this painful wound: "I have not been loved because I am at the core unlovable—and I never shall be loved." So shame at bottom would then be not anxiety, but pain, hurt, woundedness? (Ibid., 93)

This conviction that one is fundamentally unloveable originates in infancy, when the infant self is driven by the need to express (a wish for power, that is, to be able to effect desired events in the environment) and the need to perceive (a wish to merge, to be contained, safe). Failure to achieve the aims of these often conflicting drives, or an instinct horror at their strength (and therefore at their potential for damage to the loved object—"mother") produces a feeling of helplessness, against which shame acts as a defense: since shame is a prohibitor, it can restrain from "going too far" with the drives and therefore forestall the experience of defeat and helplessness. All this hidden warfare is (usually unwittingly) gazed upon by the eye of the mother, and what the infant sees in that eye will convince her that she is either loveable or not loveable.

The two risks are to offer oneself and be proved unlovable, and to merge or to conquer by sight and expression and be proved helpless. The answer to where both strands combine is clearly this: *Love resides in the face*—in its beauty, in the music of the voice and the warmth of the eye. Love is proved by the face, and so is unlovability—proved by seeing and hearing, by being seen and heard. . . . I believe the two merge in the original experience—the nourishing breast (or at least milk) and the loving face and voice. To be unlovable means not to see a responsive eye and not to hear a responding voice. . . . The helplessness of the searching eye and of

25

the cry for love is the helplessness of feeling doomed to unlovability. Function and content are one in this primary trauma; they remain combined in the affect of shame. (Ibid., 96-97)

Not a moral flaw, Wurmser believes, unloveability "is rather the sense of a fundamental, a priori cursedness, preceding self-caused guilt and shame. . . . We saw it as the abyss of primal shame" (ibid., 292-3). Ultimately, one can react to this primal shame in one of two ways: through the defense of "reaction formation," in which one becomes a perpetually provisional self, in which one's entire life is consumed with the attempt, always futile, to avoid circumstances which might activate shame. "A person's entire character can show severe constriction because he is constantly on guard against shame experiences. Not only is he shy and withdrawn in his general behavior, but his thinking and feeling may be narrowed down to certain safe areas (e.g., daydreams). Self-assured inquisitiveness, daring originality, and creativity are stifled by the pervasive sense of failure, self-consciousness and self-condemnation" (ibid., 85). But shame can be transcended through creativity and love, achieved through the relentless search for personal integrity, self-loyalty, authenticity. Put more clinically,

> Only when the theatophilic [perceptive] and delophilic [expressive, exhibitionistic] drives are under the supreme mastery of the ego's synthetic function and when the defense by denial and shame is tempered and moderated by the ego's controlling function of form-giving have we changed this archaic conflict into creativity. (Ibid., 299)

Andrew Morrison (1989), primarily influenced by the thought of Heinz Kohut, holds that regardless of the approach to shame the underlying central issue is narcissism. "Shame is an affective response to a perception of the self as flawed, and thus inevitably involves narcissism, vulnerability, and their various manifestations" (ibid., 48).

The term "narcissism" has taken on such pejorative overtones that it will be helpful to bring in Alice Miller's observation that "healthy narcissism" refers to a "person who is genuinely alive, with free access to the true self and his authentic feelings," while one suffering from a narcissistic disorder experiences the "true self's 'solitary confinement' within the prison of the false self" (Miller 1981, ix). The true self, of course, is the self which develops out of the basic core of the individual; the false self is essentially a "primitive defense mechanism" that hides the true self, "that complies with demands, that reacts to stimuli, that rids itself of instinctual experiences by having them, but that is only playing for time" (Winnicott 1975, 304-5).

Narcissism, says Morrison, demands "absolute uniqueness and sole importance to someone else," reverberates with "primitive fantasies of symbiotic merger, omnipotence, and grandiosity," and is expressed directly in claims of entitlement, defensively as "haughty aloofness and grandiosity," or affectively through responses of rage or dejection when the narcissistic demands are defeated. (Clearly, in an adult this would be considered narcissistic disorder.) Shame inevitably follows (Morrison 1989, 48-9). He agrees with Kohut that while the "primary structural defect in the nuclear self" originates in the mother's failure to act as a self-object mirroring the "child's healthy, age-appropriate exhibitionism," shame is connected more to failures to establish "compensatory structures," which in turn reflects the father's failure to respond as self-object "to the child's needs for idealization. . . . The absence of ideals and goals as a result of failure of compensatory structures is, then, a major source of self-depletion." Shame "reflects primarily the *depleted* self, having failed to receive responsiveness from the *idealized* self-object. Such a self lacks realizable ideals and is burdened by excessive and unattainable ideals and goals. . . . [Shame] reflects primarily a self-object failure to meet the age-appropriate *needs* of the self. . . ." (ibid., 75-83). The antidote to shame is "the healing response of *acceptance* of the self, despite its weaknesses, defects, and failures," (ibid., 82), which can be achieved at least in part by working with an empathic "self-object/analyst" and by "repeated transmuting internalizations"—that is, by internalizing the analyst's empathy which, if done often and deeply enough, will "transmute" into self-empathy (ibid., 75-6). Moreover, Morrison says, we can learn to live with shame by revealing secrets to appropriate others, thereby letting some of the "steam" out of the secret; by giving less power to collective assessments of ourselves; and by trying, by turning more often to our newly empathic selves, "to transform the harshness and severity of the ego ideal into a more accepting, attainable ideal self" (ibid., 182-3).

Working from what he calls "developmental self theory," a synthesis of the object-relations theory of Fairbairn and Guntrip, the interpersonal theory of Harry Stack Sullivan, and the affect theory of Silvan Tomkins, Gershen Kaufman (1989) brings together some of the perceptions we have already covered, e.g., that shame is "the affect of inferiority," that its essential nature is characterized by "sudden, unexpected exposure coupled with binding inner scrutiny" (being *seen* by both outer and inner eyes), that the shamed person feels deficient, diseased, defective. He writes almost as affectively as Wurmser:

> No other affect is more central to identity formation. . . . Like a wound made from the inside by an unseen hand, shame disrupts the natural functioning of the self. . . . The inner experience of shame is like a sickness within the self, a sickness of the soul. (Ibid., 5-6) To live with shame is to experience the very essence or heart of the self as wanting. Shame is invariably alienating, isolating, and deeply disturbing. . . . The excruciating observation of the self . . . this torment of self-consciousness, becomes so acute as to create a binding, almost paralyzing effect. (Ibid., 18)

Kaufman asserts that shame is "potentially present from birth" (ibid., 30) and that it begins as a "largely wordless experience" predating the "attainment of formal operational thought in the Piagetian sense" (ibid., 19). In his view, however, it is not a primary affect but an "affect auxiliary" which comes into play only when one of two primary positive affects, interest or enjoyment, has been activated, expectations along the lines of interest or enjoyment have been created, and those expectations are not filled—"are suddenly exposed as wrong" (ibid., 31). These affects are rooted in the physical self:

> Affects are sets of muscular, glandular, and skin receptor responses located in the face (and also widely distributed throughout the body) that generate sensory feedback to a system that finds them either inherently "acceptable" or "unacceptable." These organized sets of responses are triggered at subcortical centers where specific "programs" for each distinct affect are stored, programs that are innately endowed and have been genetically inherited. (Ibid., 29)

I find it useful and interesting to contemplate this concept in terms of Jung's postulates of the psychoid level of the archetypes. Could it be that the limbic brain, the subcortical centers—which in the human are virtually

28

identical to those in other vertebrates—is the seat of the archetypal psyche—one could say, the place where the soul enters the body, where psyche and soma are the least distinguishable from one another?

But to return to Kaufman. In suckling, the infant's interest/enjoyment affects are activated and expectation is created. "It is not oral gratification that is primary, but rather, the visual scene of union-identification—that instead govern development" (ibid., 32). Facial gazing is thus the earliest form of communion. If the fundamental expectations are not met during this activity, shame is constellated. The interpersonal bridge is broken when expectations are exposed as wrong, and breaking the interpersonal bridge "is the critical event that activates shame. . . . The failure to fully hear, openly validate, and understand another's need by directly communicating its validity can sever the interpersonal bridge and thereby activate shame." (Ibid., 34) These are ruptures which must be repaired through physical contact.

This and subsequent repeated shame experiences produce "affect magnification," and "magnified shame is more toxic to the self, just as chronic shyness is more disturbing than momentary shyness" (ibid., 57). Over time, shame becomes internalized and with repetition becomes what Kaufman terms "character shame," a state in which one believes oneself to be unloveable and defective. Internalization, he says, can occur as a component of the affect-belief configuration (through cognitive labeling), through images of interaction patterns (e.g., being blamed for mistakes), or by internalizing the "other," usually a parent. The latter is what produces the critical inner voice.

The self by now has incorporated "scripts"—defending scripts (rage, contempt, striving for power and/or perfection, humor, denial, transfer of blame, internal withdrawal) and identity scripts, which invade the self and reproduce shame: self-blame, comparison-making, self-contempt, inner voices (ibid., 100-4). Such negative scripts result in a disowning of self and in splitting: "internal strife waged relentlessly against disowned parts of the self" (ibid., 110). Now, he writes, "the internalization and magnification of shame have created an identity, a distinctive pattern of relating to oneself, that continuously absorbs, maintains, and spreads shame. The self has become shame-bound" (ibid., 112).

Healing for the shame-bound self may be achieved by a number of methods, including: validating shame; breaking the shame spiral experientially by refocusing on some positive outside the self, most pragmatically on an external sensory experience; by making conscious the "governing scenes," the early critical events which activated shame, and reshaping them through imagery and writing; reparenting the self; reowning the disowned parts of the self; disinternalizing the severe internalized parent image by learning to reject it and listen to a different voice (ibid., 182*ff*).

Finally, Donald L. Nathanson (1992), who more rigorously than Kaufman adopts Tomkin's affect theory, reiterates some of the familiar aspects of the shame experience—e.g., the elements of exposure, sudden decreases in self-esteem, failures to live up to an ego ideal, and so forth, as well as the defense mechanisms, e.g., contempt, rage. Starting with the premise that "affect is the strictly biological portion of emotion" and that "emotion is the complex combination of an affect" with the memories of previous experiences (ibid., 49-50), he establishes his central concept, Tomkin's idea that the function of an affect is to amplify the stimulus that activated it, thereby producing motivation. Consciousness itself, Nathanson asserts, is a function of affect (ibid., 114). Thus he arrives at the conclusion that shame "is a biological system by which the organism controls its affective output so that it will not remain interested in content when it may not be safe to do so, or so that it will not remain in affective resonance with an organism that fails to match patterns stored in memory" (ibid., 140). He hypothesizes that the shame affect "involves a neurochemical, a substance secreted in the ancient subcortical portion of the brain, a compound that causes sudden widening or dilatation of the blood vessels in the brain" (ibid., 141). This substance, he believes, starts up the mechanism which causes loss of muscle tone, which in turn causes the characteristic drooping head and avoidance of eye contact. This mechanism is initially free of meaning—by which I believe he means that meaning is added as life experiences accrue, since later in the text he goes on to say that pride "is attached to the acquisition of each moiety of normal growth and development and shame is attached to any failures along the way. . . . At all stages of development reminders of one's previous (and therefore more primitive) status remain capable of activating shame" (ibid., 160). This statement is helpfully related to one he makes earlier: "All our actions are capable of being viewed along a shame/pride axis. . . . To the extent that we have grown to maturity in an atmosphere of incompetence and failure or have come to believe that our true self is a defective self, we have formed a personal identity based more on shame than pride" (ibid., 86). The possibility of extremely early onset of this formation is seen in his statement that "shame can exist before the cognitive equipment of the child can allow the mechanism of self-reflection and inner looking" (ibid., 196).

Despite the obvious diversity of approaches represented in this survey, the gap being perhaps widest between Jung and Nathanson, there are certain commonalities in the perspectives on shame:

It is generally understood to be an affect (in the case of Kaufman, an "affect auxiliary").

It is generally understood to involve sudden exposure, usually of a perceived/experienced deficit when measuring self against an ideal image of self, and the logical response to undesired exposure is *hiding*, the notion of which includes not only withdrawal or "covering up" but the most extreme form of disappearance, suicide.

This "deficiency" or deficit is widely held to be the result of empathic failure in the mother/mothering figure during infancy (but for Kohut and Morrison, shame is created by the father's failure to respond to the child's need for an idealized self-object).

It is almost without exception understood to be connected with fear.

The groundwork for shame can be laid very early in life, possibly as early as birth. (However, Wurmser [1995, 73] asserts that shame is a structure of the superego and can arise only after the Oedipal complex has been resolved.

While there is no standard taxonomy of shame, there is a tendency to recognize a "shame continuum," which is to say that shame experiences may be relatively mild and coincidental, or they may have been so pervasive and so repeated as to create a "shame-bound" or "shame-based" personality. Beyond that still, shame at its very most metastasized and toxic can result in a shame psychosis and fragmentation of the psyche. (Morrison [1989, 57] concludes that for us to register shame at all, a modicum, at least, of ego strength must be present: "When concerns of fragmentation predominate . . . patients do not have the luxury to register shame." Having experienced both the threat of that danger and shame, sometimes simultaneously, I wonder whether his assertion may not be too unequivocal.)

There is general agreement on the typical defense mechanisms, e.g.,
   contempt (projection of shame), withdrawal, splitting, disowning
   of parts of the self (creating the personal shadow).

Shame activators (e.g., the severe parental voice) become internalized,
   so that shame is not always dependent on external events or on an
   immediate social context.

Shame is life-denying.

From this survey, three things emerge to draw our attention in a special
way, particularly if we know what it is to be a shamecarrier—a term I prefer
to "shame-bound" or "shame-based," since it connotes a certain strength
and the possibility of setting down part of the burden of shame.

First, to say that shame is an affect—a view, incidentally, which Aristotle
shared with our modern psychologists—is to imply that the root has not
been uncovered, since affects always have an "efficient cause," that is, there
is always a causative factor which produces the affect. I believe most of us
who are shamecarriers mistake the affect for its efficient cause; the problem,
we think, is the affect itself. If we could just stop feeling shame, life would
somehow be restored to normalcy—we would be "cured." This is a peculiar
effect of shame, to be shamed for feeling shame, causing us to locate suffering in the very expression of suffering. And often causing us to avoid
exploring the nature and content of the affect in order to get at its root. But
if we can see the affect as an expression of something lying deep beneath it,
then we can perhaps distance the affect, endure it longer and with more ego
strength, and eventually trace it down to its meaningful origins.

One way of describing this process is that it allows us to understand
shame as symbol. Jean-Pierre Vernant's delineation of the nature of "symbol" in contradistinction to "sign" led me to this perspective.

The sign refers to something outside itself as to a known object (or
   referent). . . . The sign is determinate, circumscribes; it lends itself to
   certain precise operations; at the extreme, in technical and scientific
   language, it is simple, univocal, transparent. . . . In contrast, there is
   something "natural" and "concrete" about the symbol; it belongs, in
   part, to what it expresses. . . . It is not knowledge of another object
   but a presence in itself. Thus it does not belong to the order of intellectual comprehension, as the sign does, but rather to that of affectivity

and desire. . . . The symbol is defined as fluid, diffuse, indeterminate, complex, syncretic. In contrast to the sign, ideally univocal, the symbol is polysemic; it can become charged with a limitless number of new expressive meanings. . . . [S]ymbols possess a fluidity and freedom that enable them to shift from one form to another and to amalgamate the most diverse domains within one dynamic structure. They can efface the boundaries that normally separate the different sectors of reality and convey in the reflection of a network of mutual relationships the reciprocal effects and the interpenetration of human and social factors, natural forces, and supernatural Powers. . . . [T]he symbol is never at rest, never in a state of equilibrium. It possesses a constant impulse aiming toward something beyond what it immediately expresses. (Vernant 1990, 236-8)

Vernant speaks from the disciplines of semiotics, aesthetic philosophy, and mythography, but it seems to me his statement can be brought directly, without much "translation," into the arena of psychology. If so, it is possible to say that *sign is to guilt as symbol is to shame*. Guilt is determinate, circumscribed, lends itself to "certain precise operations" (such as codes of laws and penalties), and is usually univocal in that the experience of guilt has a known and exact referent: a law, a principle, a custom, a rule has been broken, and all elements of the event—the law, the transgressor, the transgression, and the penalty—exist within one and the same sector of reality. By contrast, shame is fluid, diffuse, indeterminate, complex, polysemic, never in a state of equilibrium, in that it can erupt unpredictably upon contact with *any* sector of reality, inner or outer, e.g., in matters or memories related to love, sexuality, intelligence, physical appearance, money, knowledge, competence, spiritual growth, capacity for insight, health, athletics, art, creativity, public speaking, one's gait, one's race, gender, nationality, age, religion, family history, and so forth. In short, it can erupt in connection with virtually any facet of human experience. Nor is shame time-specific. It can "efface the boundaries that normally separate the different sectors of reality," including the boundary of time, so that we can feel at forty-five years of age plunged into deep shame as we recollect something that happened when we were seven. Or we can experience shame without knowing why, the memory of an event having been repressed. Finally, the affect of shame is a thing-in-itself but it also belongs to what it expresses, *towards which it is always aiming*—a point which will be made clearer in the last chapter.

Second, in reviewing the literature I was struck by the odd, almost jarring juxtaposition of heavily weighted affective passages and distanced, cool, clinical diction. By this observation I am not faulting the authors; on the contrary, the probable reason for this disparity is that the authors in question are empathic but are also professionals wishing to bring to an issue all the objectivity and lucidity at their command. Nonetheless, when we encounter this kind of diction of shame: wound, searing pain, mortification, sense of degradation, total loneliness, terrifying, soul murder, horror, abyss, hellish profundity, cursedness, sickness of the soul, torment . . . and these are addressed with this kind of diction: drive restraints, empathic failures, introjected figures, reaction formation, exhibitionistic impulses, oral gratification, affect binds, scopophobia, and so forth, we can scarcely keep from asking whether this cognitive-linguistic rope ladder thrown over to shame's burning building is enough.

Nor is this to derogate the vocabulary or the clinical perspectives of the psychologies; that vocabulary is simply a set of professional "signs" (in Vernant's sense) allowing psychologists to speak to one another with something resembling mutually understood languages. Rather, I make these observations in order simply to say that something is missing, as though the *experience* of shame has been grasped well enough but the approaches to uncovering its origins, as far as they go valid to one degree or another, have not gone so far as to get at the core truth of what is fundamentally unspeakable: terror, cursedness, horror, degradation, hell. To put it very simply, those of us who have been there and have really seen where we are find it hard to accept something like "empathic failures" as the entire cause, or reparenting as a good-enough response.

Finally, I was struck during the review by another set of perceptions and diction, one which I want to segregate now to provide a connective with the main destination of this chapter. That set of references, closely related to the affective diction already mentioned, comprises two subsets, one of which has to do with the immobility produced by the shame affect. Paralysis and petrifaction are mentioned by Wurmser and Kaufman. The most extreme form of immobility, death, is implied by Neumann and Hultberg, and is specifically pointed to by Wurmser and

Nathanson, both of whom use the word "mortification," whose Latin roots "imply that shame can strike one dead" (Nathanson 1992, 19).

The other subset consists of a few unusual expressions one might rather expect to find not in the literature of psychoanalysis but in religious studies, perhaps, or in a discussion of H. P. Lovecraft or Stephen King. Wurmser (1995, 83) writes that the punishment expected by the person I am calling the shamecarrier, whether expected from within or from without, contains an *uncanny elementary force*, so uncanny and so elementary that one is led to conclude that, among other things, such a powerful punishment must have been "set up to counter an equally *dangerous* and similarly *mighty force*" (emphases mine). In discussing the basic flaw of perceived unloveability, he speaks of "the sense of a fundamental, a priori cursedness," like that encountered in Greek tragedy (ibid., 292). Kaufman (1989, 5) speaks of shame as being "like a wound made from the inside by *an unseen hand*." And Hultberg refers to an "almost indescribable fear" (1988, 116).

Logic and—for some of us—experience argue that there is only one level of reality to which this vocabulary points, signifying as it does three dominant components: terror, awe, and the threat of annihilation, the obliteration of one's existence. Such a vocabulary points beyond the natural, human sphere to the realm of the supernatural, the non-human, the archetypal; in short, to the divine. For have we not gone beyond the parameters of mere human punishment when we conceive hell as "a state of eternal shame . . . implying utter physical destruction while yet one is being kept intensively alive and conscious" (Hultberg 1988, 115), and beyond the limits of human cognition when we use the word "uncanny," with its etymological relatives implicating that which transcends the natural, material order, that which is strange, awesome, unearthly? When the experience of shame has reached this magnitude, the word "shame" is no longer an adequate signifier; we have moved beyond shame—or perhaps into shame's final and deepest modality—into *dread*, into what Rudolf Otto called "daemonic dread," which "first begins to stir in the feeling of 'something uncanny,' 'eerie,' or 'weird'" (Otto 1958, 14). We are in proximity to the *mysterium tremendum*, that ultimate numinosity which is "hidden and esoteric . . . beyond conception or understanding, extraordinary and unfamiliar" (the *mysterium*) which causes a response of "fear that is more than fear proper . . . a terror fraught with an inward shuddering" (the *tremendum*) (ibid., 13).

The Greeks had a word for this trembling awe: *aidos*. And they personified the concept in the figure of Aidos, goddess of Shame, who, as we know, was the nursemaid of Athene. With these two goddesses—once we get past the thin and superficial layer of allegory—we are in the archetypal domain. It is to them that we turn in the next chapter, to learn from them what we can before taking up again the subject of dread and its implications.

We have already looked at some of the ways in which our culture is fundamentally indebted and similar to the early Greeks'. Yet another similarity is expressed in this poignant and damning statement from philosopher Bernard Williams:

> We are in an ethical condition that lies not only beyond Christianity, but beyond its Kantian and its Hegelian legacies. We have an ambivalent sense of what human beings have achieved, and have hopes for how they might live (in particular, in the form of a still powerful ideal that they should live without lies). We know that the world was not made for us, or we for the world, that our history tells no purposive story, and that there is no position outside the world or outside history from which we might hope to authenticate our activities. We have to acknowledge the hideous costs of many human achievements that we value, including this reflective sense itself, and recognise that there is no redemptive Hegelian history or universal Leibnizian cost-benefit analysis to show that it will come out well enough in the end. In important ways, we are, in our ethical situation, more like human beings in antiquity than any Western people have been in the meantime. More particularly, we are like those who, from the fifth century and earlier, have left us traces of a consciousness that had not yet been touched by Plato's and Aristotle's attempts to make our ethical relations to the world fully intelligible. (Williams 1993, 166)

Because of this dire and horrific commonality, enhanced by a shared imaginal field, we may hope to find a deeply personal meaning in Walter Burkert's provocative observation:

The modern historian of religion may speak of "archetypal figures of reality," but in the Greek, locution and ideation [of the deities] is structured in such a way that an individual personality appears that has its own plastic being. This cannot be defined, but it can be known, and such knowledge can bring joy, help, and salvation. (Burkert 1985, 183)

Chapter Two

Aidos, Athene, and the Gorgon

What we call pathology the Greeks experienced as mythology. So also when Demeter "lets herself go," as we would say, "disguising her beauty," as Homer says. The loony bins of America are full of people who disguise their beauty, for one reason or another, as surely as the roadsides in antiquity were crowded with ancient versions of the same. But while this condition seems "sick" to us, a matter of bad "mental" health, it seemed sacred to the Greeks. They had a goddess to guide them through it.
    — Charles Boer, in Introduction to *The Homeric Hymns*

Perhaps no three figures from Greek mythology are more centrally related to shame and dread than the triad made up of Aidos, Athene, and Medousa. Let us begin our exploration with the one most recently mentioned, Aidos, whose relationship to shame is self-evident.

As a goddess, Aidos (pronounced "eye-dahss" in ancient Greek, in modern Greek as "eh-dahss," the same "e" as in "red") did not live with the Olympian deities but ranged the earth. This assignment seems reasonable in view of the fact that it was only humans, not the gods, who felt or needed the experience of shame. Aidos had an altar on the Athenian akropolis near the temple of Athene, and a reserved seat at the theatre of Dionysos, indicating how close she was to the heart of the community. Little more is known about her, except that like all the deities she was sometimes depicted as winged.

As a concept, *aidos* is difficult to translate; we have no precise English equivalent. In modern Greek, the word means pretty much what "shame" popularly means to us now—disgrace, dishonor, infamy. It can also denote that one is debauched, depraved, sordid, greedy, indecent, or—somewhat paradoxically—shameless; it can also refer to obscenity. For these modern denotations, however, the old Greeks had another word, *aischyne*. *Aidos* was reserved for something more subtle and, from Homer on, was directly linked with one's relationship to the collective. It has variously been described as respect for public opinion (Dodds 1951, 17); respect for honor, one of the primary necessary conditions for a moral existence (Snell 1953, 167); as the sense of duty (Jaeger 1945, 1: 57); as consciousness of moral obligation (ibid., 420); as "a modest bashfulness, a quiet respectful awe within nature and toward nature" (Hillman 1979, x1vi).

Clearly, regardless of variations in the definition, *aidos* was inextricably tied to the collective's prevailing ideas of what constituted honor, respect, duty. These definitions changed during the several centuries between Homer and Democritus. To track those changes in full would take us on a complex path too far away from our main concern here, but a brief excursion is cogent.

For Homeric man, the citizen of the early archaic age, the highest good was the esteem of his fellows, and the "strongest moral force . . . is not fear of god, but respect for public opinion, *aidos*. . . . In such a society, anything which exposes a man to the contempt or ridicule of his fellows, which causes him to 'lose face,' is felt as unbearable" (Dodds 1951, 17-8). "Loss of face" always involved diminution of one's honor, which could be brought about by behaving in a way which deviated from fairly clear collective standards, putting oneself outside society's norms. Such an act might be a failure to honor the gods, which was "principally a matter of observing their cult." Piety was expressed in behavior, "in acts of respect toward the gods [and] was literally a matter of 'respect,' not love" (Parker 1989, 255). The idea of loving god, or at least the word for it, does not appear until much later, with Aristotle (Dodds 1951, 35). Perhaps it was because this world was well ordered (at least, by comparison with its predecessor Dark Age) that the rules for behavior in it could be so clear. Writes Bruno Snell,

> The commandment: "Respect the gods" was interpreted in two ways: first, people should not commit acts of open *asebeia*, religious transgressions [a crime for which the death penalty could be demanded: an outrage committed against something sacred—stealing dedicatory gifts, mutilating statues, polluting a temple, betraying the secrets

of the Mysteries]; and secondly, they ought to participate in the rites
of the official cult. (Snell 1953, 27)

So impiety was one way of losing face. The other, equally serious, was to perform a base act, an act beneath society's standards of good and which resulted in a loss of *time*, honor. We have to remember that *time* did not yet denote an internalized sense of one's ethical integrity but something closer to "public honors," which for the early Greek aristocracy was apparently an almost palpable possession, like gold or land. It may be difficult for us to grasp a time and world view in which theology and morality were not linked, since they are so closely tied in our own. For Homeric man, there was no theology as we know it, nor was there "sin" as we know it. "Man was not for the Greeks a sinful being in need of redemption," writes Robert Parker, and "piety was not a matter of perpetual moral endeavor under the watchful guidance of conscience" (1989, 255). Instead, the ethical life, the pursuit of the "good," was a matter of acting in such a way that one was seen by one's peers as "useful, proficient, and capable of vigorous action" (Snell 1953, 158). To be virtuous is to achieve abundance of material possessions and honor, to have a reputation for nobility, prowess, and success, and to "realize one's nature, and one's wishes, to perfection . . . this also entails that he is good in the eyes of others, for the notions and definitions of goodness are plain and uniform: a man appears to others as he is" (ibid.).

The will to achieve one's nature to perfection was summed up in the concept of *arete*, which in its oldest meaning referred to nobility, a "combination of proud and courtly morality with warlike valour" (Jaeger 1945, 1: 5). And central to nobility was *aidos*, a sense of duty to the gods and in the community, but also of the duty of others towards oneself. For these early Greeks, achieving one's nature to perfection did not mean anything remotely close to what we mean today by, for example, individuation; one's nature was identified with the nature of the society to which one belonged—in this case, the aristocracy—and to achieve that nature to perfection was to achieve the ideals of the class to which one belonged.

In the Homeric period, then, *aidos* was both a sense of duty and a respect for honor, and "shame" was a consequence of failing in either sphere in the eyes of one's peers. This is succinctly and pointedly reflected in the fact that the battle cry of the men of the *Iliad* was a single word, "*Aidos!*"

Failure meant removal from the collective, or from its good opinion, by being deprived of honors due, by failing to strive for *arete*, by failing to respect and abide by the dictates of the community.

As the Greeks edged towards what we now call the classical period, ideas about man's relationship to the community and to the gods changed, as did perspectives on crime, impiety, honor, and *aidos*. With the coalescing of city-states and a more defined political structure came increasing codification of the laws; it was in written law and legal usage (*nomos*) that the Greeks of the later archaic period believed they had found a reliable criterion for right and wrong. The general idea of righteousness acquired a palpable content: it consisted in obedience to the laws of the state. The city-state (*polis*), explains Jaeger,

> is the sum of all its citizens and of all the aspects of their lives.
> . . . From it are derived all the norms which govern the lives of
> its citizens. Conduct that injures it is bad, conduct that helps it
> is good. . . . Even the most intimate acts of the private life and
> the moral conduct of its citizens are by law prescribed and lim-
> ited and defined. . . . Law was the most universal and permanent
> form of Greek moral and legal experience. . . . The early city-
> state was, in the eyes of its citizens, the guarantee of all the ideals
> which made life worth living. (Jaeger 1945, 1: 108-9)

We may be inclined to respond to this with the thought that no culture was ever more thickly collective. Yet language underscores the collectivity of our own and illuminates the difficulties, even the opprobrium, attached to departure from our collective: communal, public man in Greece was the *politikos*; the separate, private man the *idiotes*. These were clean, nonjudgmental distinctions. Our own culture took the root *idios*, which meant simply "personal" or "separate" and gave us pejoratives such as idiot, idiocy, idiosyncrasy. This is what our collective secretly thinks of people who deviate from it, however much it may tout the virtues of individualism.

Important as the *nomos* was, the weight of religious injunctions was far from gone. Indeed, during this period the old idea of *ate*—or possession by a deity, "the daemonic power of infatuation" (Jaeger 1945, 1: 48)—still obtained, and to it were added the daunting ideas of *phronos*, the jealousy

41

and retaliation of the gods if one amassed too many honors and material goods, and *hybris*, which in Homer's day simply denoted a concrete violation of the law but now referred to the arrogance of the man who forgets that human power and ambition are inherently limited. "Know thyself," the famous Delphic dictum, was not an invitation to self-understanding or introspection but the ultimate reminder not to try to exceed the bounds of human nature—a sort of cosmological boundary setting. Add to these the prospect of unintentionally, unwittingly committing a transgression and becoming "polluted," a condition more horrific now than it had been in Homer's time, when purification was a relatively simple procedure. Now it could mean not only being cast out from the community but also being the source of calamity for the whole community through *miasma*, the power of contagion. Writes Jean-Pierre Vernant,

> In the case of murder, for example, the *miasma* is embodied in all the beings or objects that are involved in the crime: the murderer, the weapon, the blood, and the victim. If the crime is of a directly sacrilegious nature, the uncleanliness . . . may even embrace an entire territory, causing the land to be infertile, the herds to be barren, and the children to be born deformed. (Vernant 1990, 134-5)

With this shift in mind, Dodds (1951) invites his reader to compare Homer's Oidipus, who was allowed to continue his reign over Thebes until his death, with the later Oidipus of Sophokles, who is cast out of society because of his unspeakable defilement.

Not until later, in the classical period, would intentionality become a factor in the assessment of responsibility and guilt: a man's act may be the result of possession by a *daimon*, over which he has no control, but he is nonetheless required to bear responsibility for it. This may seem simplistic and primitive, but it foreshadows today's psychological view that we must ultimately take responsibility for unconsciousness—our inflations, projections, shadow.

So life for the ancient Greek aristocrat must have been fraught with pitfalls. We can imagine him walking the exceedingly narrow path which threaded among the jealousy of the gods, the acquisition or loss of honor, the hazards of aggregating too much success and too little, accusations of impiety, violations of the law, fear of being swept into misbehavior by Ate, of transgressing when one does not intend to transgress, of being defiled and cast out. Punishment for transgressions is the same with and without intentionality, and he who transgresses bears a double burden, of being despised by the gods—else why would they inflict *ate* upon him?—and shame before men. It might even be that he has not transgressed but his father did, or his grandfather; he inherits this moral debt along with the family land, and he, or his son or grandson, will be punished for the old violation. Sooner or later, the debt exacted payment. In this way, "the idea of cosmic justice, which . . . provided a sanction for the new civic morality [was] . . . associated with a primitive conception of the family"—a misfortune for the Greeks, says Dodds, "for it meant that the weight of religious feeling and religious law was thrown against the emergence of a true view of the individual as a person, with personal rights and personal responsibilities" (Dodds 1951, 34).

It would be some time before this new view would emerge. When it did, it was accompanied by a sense of man's majestic courage which enabled him to endure despite the crushing weight of a religion of fear. Its emergence was due almost entirely to the work of the philosophers, who more than any other group changed the mentality of archaic Greece, making possible the rise of democracy and the significantly revised importance of the individual in the classical age.

From Thales in the sixth century onwards, the philosophers began to fertilize the loam of the Greek mind with ideas which would substantially modify the Hellenic view of man and the divine. Now begins the shaping of the cultural achievements which we think of today as quintessentially Greek and which found their highest expression in Periclean Athens: in politics, democracy and respect for individual freedom; in the arts, a love of proportion and beauty of form, enjoying the fullest support of the government and the citizenry; in the ethos, high value placed on intellectual powers, rationalism, humanism, and the Golden Mean. So strong is this ideal image that it persists, even as part of our own myth, despite our knowledge that Greek "democracy" did not extend to women and slaves; that artistic achievement owed more to Athens' tyrants than to its more liberal leaders (Jaeger 1945, 1: 229); the Golden Mean, moderation in all things, says Kitto, was valued so highly by the Greek precisely "because he was so prone to extremes" (Kitto 1960, 252); and "individual freedom" referred not to our concept but to a *public* freedom, the freedom to choose among the demands of the religious association, the group of relatives, the family, the *deme*, the phratry (a brotherhood), and "so to escape any particular dominant form of social patterning" (O. Murray 1989, 204).

Free as he may have been to choose among these demands, the citizen must have had to possess perfect clarity about how to make that choice.

> The Greek in the classical era . . . thought that political morality and personal morality were practically identical: since the state was the sole source of all moral standards, and it was difficult to see what other moral code could exist apart from the code of the state, the law of the community in which the individual lived and had his being. A purely private moral code, without reference to the state, was inconceivable to the Greeks. . . . In the fifth century there were only two possibilities: either the law of the state was the highest standard for human life and coincided with the divine government of the universe, in which case a man was a citizen, no more and no less; or else the standards of the state conflicted with those established by nature or god, so that man could not accept them, in which case he ceased to be a member of the political community, and the very foundations of his life dissolved, unless he could find some certainty in the eternal order of nature. (Jaeger 1945, 1: 326)

Where we may see in this outlook implications of fascism, to the classical Greek mind it was a demonstrable and sensible foundation of a world view derived from pure reason and empiricism. There are invisible forces, that view held, which operate in the visible world and which obtain both in nature and in the human social domain. Those forces often operate and interrelate through tension and opposition—which is to say, through conflict—and as in nature they achieve a state of equilibrium, so in human society they must operate or be made to operate in accordance with the ideal of *isonomia*, in which power and authority remain at the center and are not allowed to be held by a single individual or a privileged majority. "The Greek image of the world is fundamentally geometrical in character. The cosmos is imagined in spatial terms. The order that governs it is egalitarian rather than hierarchical. It assumes a balanced distribution between contrary powers so that none of these can come to dominate the others" (Vernant 1990, 97).

Underlying this concept is the perception, still holding in the classical age, that the divine is present in the human environment, and that the same powers inform all aspects of life. Thus the laws governing social organization and behavior were still radically connected to the laws governing the cosmos and one's religious behavior; they derived from the same source, and that source was to some degree intelligible, knowable by the human mind.

> This is not to say that the Greeks confused everything together and that theirs was a kind of primitive mentality where everything participated in everything else. The Greeks made distinctions in their religious thought, but not the same ones we make. They distinguished in the cosmos between different types of powers—multiple forms of power that could take action on every level of reality . . . making interventions within man himself as well as in society, in nature, and in the Beyond. (Vernant 1990, 103-4)

Ethics, then, which in the strict sense of the term began only with Socrates, consists of a "system of transcendental values considered as universally applicable truths from which it should be possible to deduce the various courses of behavior suited to particular circumstances" (ibid., 95). Primary among those transcendental values were those of Piety, Courage, Beauty, and Justice, understood in the context of an ordered and balanced social structure and the cosmos which was its matrix. For the individual to participate in that structure (that is, to be a citizen) and therefore to help maintain order and balance, he needed only to be in accord with the truths set out in the laws, the *nomos*. To violate the law is not only to wrong an individual or to throw the social structure out of shape but is to risk a distortion of the sacred order of the universe. The guilty party must then pay whatever penalty or debt is needed to restore that order. We see the same idea at work nearly two millenia later, in *Hamlet*: "The time is out of joint; O cursed spite,/That ever I was born to set it right!"

What an enormous burden of potential culpability this view laid on the individual, and what a magnitude of shame it opened up. Where in the Homeric period one risked loss of honor and the respect of one's peers, and in the later archaic period one might become a source of contagious pollution, now one could be the reason for the entire cosmos being thrown out of kilter. Now we can see more clearly how Homer's Oidipus could retain his Theban crown where the later Oidipus of Sophokles was a reviled exile: his unwitting act had injured the universal order.

Yet another new thought places new responsibility on the individual. Toward the end of the fifth century the laws begin to acknowledge the relevance of motive, and one's inner life as well as one's outer behavior comes into question: "clean hands are not enough—the heart must be clean also" (Dodds 1951, 37). This introduction of intentionality could be possible only with a growing recognition of the importance of the individual, the reality of the individual discrete from his role as an element in the collective. One of the results of this shift was a revision of the ethical code, so that by the late classical, Democritus could postulate a new definition of *aidos*. What had been earlier in his lifetime respect for the law he replaced with "the wonderful idea of *aidos* which a man feels for himself" (Jaeger 1945, 1:330). One must be "pure" in one's inner life as well as in the outer, and honor is now held to be the outer image of inner value.

Democritus' view of *aidos* may have had its roots in the Orphic movement of the sixth century, which promulgated the idea of an immortal soul which must be kept absolutely pure during its sojourn on earth, along with the precept that the individual is responsible for conducting himself in such a way that purity will be sustained. This idea also crept into the new interest in the soul and its central importance to the revised ideal of *arete*. "In the process, the Athenian mind becomes anthropocentric and humanism is born" (Jaeger 1945, 1:280)—not the emotion of love for all other members of society, called *philanthropia*, but intellectual search for and interest in the true nature of man. So, of course, is a revision of the tragic view. "To know oneself is thus for Sophokles to know man's powerlessness; but it is also to know the indestructible and conquering majesty of suffering humanity" (ibid., 284).

The idea of the *aidos* which a man feels for himself is one which never again fades from awareness. The idea of self-respect separate from collective evaluations and judgment is evident in Plato (whose youth overlapped Democritus' last years), specially in the *Symposium*, and in Aristotle, who discourses at some length both on *aidos* and on *aischyne* in the *Nichomachean Ethics*. There we read that *arete* can be sought only through ennobled self-love, "the highest kind of self-love which makes man reach out towards the highest *arete*: through which he 'takes possession of the beautiful,'" for Aristotle primarily acts of moral heroism. "A man who loves himself will always be ready to sacrifice himself for his friends or his country, to abandon possessions and honours in order to 'take possession of the beautiful'" (*Ethics*, 1169; W.D. Ross trans.).

Here we see both the echoes of the old Homeric aristocratic ideals of nobility and of Democritus' notion of *aidos* for one's self, surely related to self-respect and to "ennobled self-love." Martha Nussbaum (1980, 429, n. 10) neatly sums up the entire Greek ethic in one sentence: "Not only Plato and Aristotle but also the bulk of Greek literature, which ascribes great importance to the sense of shame, attacks the vice of shamelessness, and connects the avoidance of shame with excellence of character and action in accordance with shared norms."

This brings us to a distinction which is crucial to our understanding of Athene's connection with shame as *aidos* and to the exploration of our own involvement with shame. For the moment, I want only to make that distinction clear; its usefulness in our psychology will be looked at later. To summarize, from Homer to Democritus and beyond we have looked at the concept of *aidos*. It has been variously defined—in Homer, as a sense of duty and honor and respect for public opinion, in the later archaic and early classical ages as respect for the law, and in the late classical and Hellenistic periods, increasingly as respect (love) for self. Failures of *aidos* during all those centuries produced *aischyne*, the affect of shame, the fullest examination of which we do not see until Aristotle.

Perhaps even from this brief overview of Greek moral-ethical attitudes and cosmology it is possible to understand what an essential role *aidos* played in the stability and integrity of Greek life. As Snell says of *aidos* in the secular form it took from Homer forward, it was "a mighty pillar in the structure of civilized humanity" (Snell 1953, 167). From Homer to Perikles, *aidos* provided the constraints which allowed, one might say, for the preservation and conservation of all that was most cherished by the Greeks—honor, justice, beauty, courage, reason, balance, proportion; without *aidos*, one imagines, the culture would have been in a state of collective *aischyne*.

But before Democritus, before the Milesian philosophers, even before Homer, *aidos* had a different meaning from any of those we have uncovered. According to Snell, *aidos* originated "as the reaction which the holy excites" in a human being. Thus it was a religious, not a social or legal, element which informed the Homeric "respect for parents, reverence for a king, and reverence even for a beggar or suppliants who have no rights but

stand under the special protection of the deity." *Aidos*, Snell says, "perpetuates the authority and hierarchic order of an earlier society whose venerable
customs were regarded as sacred, as a work of the gods. . . . "

> Thus a deep conservatism is the key-note of the calls to *aidos* and of the
> injunctions against "budging" the holy. The *aidos* of religion is the most
> powerful agency known in the early age for imposing inhibitions upon
> an agent: witness the action of the goddess who restrained Achilles from
> indulging his savage desire and impairing the sacred bonds of reverence.
> (Snell 1953, 167-8)

Likewise, Vernant points out that the concept of *aidos* (along with other
concepts such as *hybris*) was originally mythical in significance and was
part of religious procedures which "with the mythical symbolism connected with them, developed into a juridical system" (Vernant 1990, 243).
The original nature of the term can be surmised from its relationship to
its Sanskrit root, *ide*, to revere.

Democritus' *aidos* closes a circle, for with his concept of reverence for
and towards self, he returns to the individual, personal experience, the only
locus for the "reaction which the holy excites," which is to say for the experience of the numinous. This experience, like that of respect for the self,
may be had together with others—that is, simultaneously among
individuals in assembly—but it cannot ever be in the strict sense a *collective*
experience, nor can it ever be fully communicated to another. Both forms
of *aidos*, the sacred and the individual, take place deep within the individual psyche and, in the end, are wholly independent of collective
definitions and norms.

That *aidos* originally denoted man's reaction to the holy sets the concept back in time, certainly to pre-Homeric time and, one can argue, back
to the Greek Bronze Age, when religion was still at its most chthonian,
most numinous, when the experience of the holy was surrounded with
mystery, not with reason or law. Paradoxically, this understanding also brings
the concept forward, taking it out of narrow temporal and geographical-
cultural confines, a movement which frees us to see its kinship to our own
experience. In other words, *aidos* can be set in the archetypal realm and can
be explored and understood as a constant in the human condition. Here,
on this bridge of time, one footing in the Bronze Age, the other in our

contemporary psyches, is where we shall discover the central relevance of Athene—the original Athene, the chthonian Athene of the Gorgon—in our lives. Our first task in making that discovery is to let our imagination enter the mythical world—to "mythologize." Our second is to "demythologize" and, to paraphrase Vernant, make the earlier experience a dimension of modern thought.

AIDOS AND ATHENE

Now that we have reasonably well in hand our various definitions of *aidos*, we have part of the answer to our question about why Aidos, goddess of Shame, should be linked with Athene, who in her popular image may seem so far removed from any connection with shame as we know it today. I say "part of the answer" because it is not difficult to see immediately why the stereotyped Athene—the Father's Daughter, the Zeus-sprung goddess of Reason and goddess of War, the "archetypal person within the fantasy of normality" (Hillman 1980, 27)—would get attached to archaic and classical notions of *aidos*. We can see how this Athene came to be said to have had Aidos for her nursemaid, for it was during the archaic period that the law, the *nomos*, became the absolute standard for right conduct. Athene, as the protector *par excellence* of the city-state of Athens and by now irrevocably shaped as a daughter of the patriarchy, would necessarily be linked with the forces which most held the *polis* intact. In this light (but perhaps only in this light), Hillman was probably correct in describing Athene as normative, as "representing the point of view of the cultural canon" (op. cit.).

But what of the Athene who had been part of the old matriarchal Chthonic religion, of which *aidos* as aweful reverence must have been a profound and central part? That there is such an Athene, a sort of Ur-Athene, is almost a commonplace among scholars of ancient Greek religion, none of whom, however, has gone to any great lengths to demonstrate how that conclusion was reached. My own forays into the question produced a discussion too indirectly related to include in the main text but too important to leave out altogether; accordingly, much of it has been relegated to chapter notes and an appendix, where the interested reader may follow my investigations and reasoning. Here, in the main text, I have included my conclusions about her "personality" (I speak of her as though she were an historical person—which she *is*, but psychologically historical), along with some distilled explanations for those conclusions. They delineate a person whose richness and complexity spill over such narrow containers as "battle maiden" or goddess of Reason," but do allow themselves to be summarized under three general aspects: the nature and range of her sense of relatedness; the quality of her mind; and the nature and range of her creativity.

ATHENE'S SENSE OF RELATEDNESS

Almost without exception Athene enters into relationships with an astonishingly clear sense of boundaries. She remains virginal, one-unto-herself, guardian of the inner world who is nonetheless capable of indefatigable action in the outer world. With this at the core of her personality, she is able to call on both her feminine and masculine aspects, to be the ultimate, conscious androgyne; she can be tender and responsive as well as just and objective. This, in turn, allows her to appear to humans in forms they can understand, a knack which enables Athene to provide what is needed psychologically. She can stir to courage, to restraint, to justice, to patience.

And she can relate to principle as well as to persons, a capacity which keeps her "on course," not blown here and there by prevailing winds, not captive of affect or of collective restrictions. That freedom permits her willingness to step away from the collective if the situation warrants, as she does when she lets Prometheus enter Olympos to steal fire for the use of humans, as she does when she installs the Erinyes on the Akropolis at the end of Aischylos' *Eumenides*.

It is notable that she never strives for perfection, nor does she urge it upon others; she goes for *what works*. Perhaps it is this freedom from perfectionism which allows her from time to time to express, without shame, her "shadow side," to reveal her anger, jealousy, pique, as may be seen in the tales of her reactions to Arachne and to Aphrodite when they are caught usurping her prerogatives around weaving.[1] Equally notable is the absence of sentimentality in her actions and speech, as seen in the epic literature.

For the most part, these assessments have been drawn from fresh readings of the *Iliad* and the *Odyssey*, where her capacity for mentoring, guiding, sensitivity to human emotions—e.g., in her relationships to Akhilleus, Odysseus, Telemachos, Menelaos, Penelopeia—are manifestly clear. This capacity may be understood as characterizing one of her central roles, that of companion-guardian, harking back to her original and primary status as house guardian, therefore benevolent guardian of the family, in the Minoan culture and later in the Minoan-Mycenaean. (This aspect, of course, culminates in her function with which we are most familiar, as guardian of the city-state of Athens.) From the *Iliad* we may remember best the times when Athene stirs the attack, guides the spear, shrieks the battle cry. Perhaps we forget, because they are less dramatic, the actions which on inspection prove to predominate in her behavior: her calming counsel to Akhilleus; the many times she deflects spears and arrows to prevent injury or death to her beloved Mycenaeans, as she does in the case of Menelaos, "the way a mother would keep a fly from settling on a child when he is happily asleep" (4, 151; Fitzgerald trans.), a simile which bespeaks home and tenderness and is one of the textual relics of Athene's earlier role. Many times she instills not rage but courage, answers prayers, sends good omens, creates light so her men may see, mists so the enemy cannot; reassures and steadies. Aias even calls her a "coddling mother" to Odysseus (23, 900; Fitzgerald trans.). Throughout the epic she is no fiercer than any natural mother would instinctively be in protecting her children.

Equally important is her aspect as mother, a vestige, no doubt, of her descent from the Great Mother. "Athene, always armed, belongs to the innermost centre of the house, with her lamp and her work at the loom" (Burkert 1985, 218); we may take this image as emblematic of her motherly interests in general. It is a central aspect of Athene which we have lost, after nearly two millenia of emphasis on her role as virgin and champion of the male. "Virgin" she was—just as many other goddesses were, surprisingly even Hera and Aphrodite—but most importantly, she was virgin in Esther Harding's sense: she remained always "one-unto-herself" (Harding 1971); the "innermost centre" of her house remained inviolate and free. Burkert tells us that "In the case of goddesses, the relationship to sexuality is more difficult [than it is in the case of gods]; since the female role is generally described as passive, as being tamed, *damenai*, it accords ill with the role of the Mistress. Consequently, it is as untamed virgins that Artemis and Athena enjoy their special power. . . . " (Burkert 1985, 183).

This psychological form of virginity does not preclude motherhood. "Athena, like Artemis, may demand periods of service in her temple from young girls; for her priestess she requires a mature woman who is past the works of Aphrodite. In all this marriage and sexuality are not excluded but presupposed" (ibid., 221). Indeed, in iconography and in myth we repeatedly find allusions to Athene's essential maternity. Usually, it is expressed in the larger sense: she is the protector of the city, of the anchorage, of the road; she is "Athene of Abundance," Kurotrophos, Nurturer of Children; and Athene Promachus, protector of heroes. But even as Promachus, which on the face of it binds her to the masculine, she is playing out an ancient and pre-Olympian role: her relationships with, e.g., Theseus, Herakles, Akhilleus, Odysseus, in which she comes to their aid, defends them, rescues them, gives them counsel, manifest a carryover of the very ancient divine mother-son configuration. Writes Harrison, "she is the foster-mother of heroes after the old matriarchal fashion" (Harrison 1991, 300). To these heroes we may add the name of Erichthonios, whom Burkert describes as being, "in the specifically Athenian tradition," the *de facto* child of Hephaistos and Athene (Burkert 1985, 220).[2] Athene was also said not only to have adopted but to have suckled Iacchos, the title of Dionysos as he was known in the Eleusinian Mysteries. Here, as elsewhere, Athene is linked to the chthonic, to mysticism, to vegetative renewal, and indirectly to Demeter, the quintessential maternal.

But it is in the *Odyssey*, composed one or two generations later than the *Iliad*, that Athene's gentler relationship skills are most evident. There she is undiluted tender concern, wisdom, discretion, and sensitivity as she protects the family of Odysseus, counsels and stimulates Telemachos to wise action, comforts Penelopeia, and enables the hero's return to Ithaka, where she assists him in the decimation of the suitors. At the end, when all is restored, she calls for reconciliation and an end to strife—not the desires of a war goddess. Every aspect of her relationship to the royal family evinces maternal solicitude.

Athene is sometimes even credited with being the mother of the human race. One story tells that she and Erichthonios seeded the earth with people, another that when Prometheus fashioned men of clay and water, it was Athene who breathed life into them. Her maternal solicitude is remembered even in the classical age, as in the *Eumenides*, when Athene instructs the Erinyes to guard the seed of the race.

THE QUALITY OF ATHENE'S MIND

Athene combines the direct, almost instinctive, innate wisdom we associate with the feminine (as Sophia) with the strategic, discursive, linear intelligence we associate with the masculine but which could also be understood as the *yang* aspect of the feminine. She repeatedly evinces clarity, clear-sightedness, independent thought, pragmatism, directness, a capacity for seeing more than one point of view, and the utmost vigilance; she is alert, watchful. She pays attention, reflects on what she sees, and undertakes what she judges to be the best course of action.

Athene's yoking of feminine and masculine energies emerges from close readings of the literature as one of her most striking attributes. From the perspective of archetypal psychology, the goddess can usefully be seen as an expression of a certain wholeness, of a woman who has discovered her *yang* aspects—what May Sarton called "that great sanity, that sun, the feminine power" (Sarton 1978, 193). It can also be seen as an expression of a woman who knows how to relate to those powers, how to deploy them. Jane Ellen Harrison, writing around the turn of the century, suggested that the Athenians had made Athene into a "sexless thing" (Harrison 1991, 302), but where Harrison saw no sexuality, no gender, there may instead be *all* sexuality, both genders, perfect androgyny. It is not even too far-fetched to speak of Athene as a cross-dresser, wearing as she so often does the *peplos* of the Greek woman but also a helmet, carrying lance and shield but often the spindle, which reminds us of her association with the very ancient role of weaver, spinner of destiny, always emblematic of the Great Mother, who "sprang originally from the ground, and was bi-sexual" (Rose 1991, 170).[3]

Religious practice and societal views of the early Greeks also afford a way of understanding Athene's cross-gender imagery. It was held that females fulfilled their nature through marriage, males through warfare.

> Thus a girl who refuses marriage, thereby also renouncing her "femininity," finds herself to some extent forced toward warfare, and paradoxically becomes the equivalent of a warrior. This is the situation in myth of females like the Amazons and, in a religious context, of goddesses such as Athena: Their status as a warrior is linked to their condition as a *parthenos* who has sworn everlasting virginity. It could even be said that this deviation . . . gives a special intensity to warrior values when these are embodied in a girl. They cease, in a way, to be merely relative or confined to a single sex, and become "total." (Vernant 1990, 34)

As divine androgyne, Athene transcends the ordinary categories, breaks through the stalemate of a binary order, and comes to represent the dynamic freedom and opportunity of the unexpected "third." Cross-dressing in an individual who has achieved some degree of wholeness, who has at once yoked together and transcended gender binarism, is not pathological transvestism; it is the outward expression of an inner, productive, tension-bearing union, which is always highly potent. Such sublime androgyny—the inner marriage of what we call, for lack of better terms, the feminine and masculine energies—does not develop by cleaving to one side of the gender dyad. It suggests the presence of an extraordinary capacity for walking the middle way, for balance—again, reflecting the mediating "third" which transcends polarities. Joseph Henderson comments:

> The creative power of the feminine spirit, as virgin, antedates or transcends the idea of hierogamy since it approximates the original "neuter creative wholeness" of the primordial state. Here extremes meet, since this is also the way of the savior through whom the human material state of being may be redeemed. (Henderson and Oakes 1991, 30)

And Mircea Eliade, writing from within the discipline of comparative religion, comments,

> The phenomenon of divine androgyny is very complex: it signifies more than the co-existence—or rather coalescence—of the sexes in the divine being. Androgyny is an archaic and universal formula for the expression of *wholeness*, the co-existence of the contraries, or *coincidentia oppositorum*. More than a state of sexual completeness and autarchy, androgyny symbolizes the perfection of a primordial, non-conditioned state. . . . *But androgyny extends even to divinities who are pre-eminently masculine or feminine.* This means that androgyny has become a general formula signifying *autonomy, strength, wholeness*; to say of a divinity that it is androgyne is as much as to say that it is the ultimate being, the ultimate reality. . . . One might call this primordial state *a neuter and creative wholeness.* (Eliade 1960, 174-9)

There is evidence that this primordial state was present in the goddess from earliest antiquity into classical times, although it manifests in very different ways in the chthonian and the Olympian colorations. Thus Athene Skiras, whose temple was at the Athenian harbor at Phaleron, "had some connection with a demigod Skoris . . . and had to do with primitive fertility cults, processions of fruit, transvestism, etc." (Levi 1971, 1:11, n. 16). In the classical age there is perhaps no better example than her role in the *Eumenides*, in which as first president of the first Areiopagos she casts the vote which acquits Orestes. Often cited as an example of Athene's loyalty to the patriarchy, not only because of her vote but because of her speech, "I am always for the male with all my heart, and strongly on my father's side" (737-8; Lattimore trans.), the playwright's text also has Athene acknowledge, with a sensitivity bordering on tenderness, the rights and powers of the old order embodied in the Erinyes. Moreover, she charges the Erinyes with the welfare and continuity of the human race—again, motherly concern on Athene's part. Her respect for the potency of the Erinyes is evinced by the fact that she must call on the goddess Persuasion to guide her speech, and by her fear, until the very end of the play, that she may be unable to keep the Erinyes from unleashing their wrath.

Specially important for present purposes is that Orestes was caught in a sanction bind. In part, this is what the play is about, "adjudication between chthonian and Olympian views" (Hadas 1960, 42). The old order decreed that matricide was the worst possible crime, the new that the greatest evil was the killing of a king. This is a wonderfully pure expression not only of a radical culture shift but of the devaluation of the feminine. Orestes is caught precisely in the collision between the two orders, on that tensive edge where equivocation, averting of the eyes, muddy allegiances, pretense, dualism, are no longer possible. In a way, even though she is divine, Athene is caught in the same bind. But she finds a way out without further bloodshed, without dishonor to the chthonian, and with utmost realism about the power of the new patriarchy. Once more, her pragmatism and ability to balance, to mediate, are foremost, and her concern is essentially maternal. "My ambition/for good wins out in the whole issue," she declares (974-5; Lattimore trans.). "Even when new and better ways are introduced," writes

55

Moses Hadas, "the old and familiar are not abolished but subli-
mated to new usefulness in an altered role" (ibid., 45).

Athene's ability to effect reconciliation between the chthonian and the
Olympian led Hillman to describe her as "normative."

> Athene is necessity moved from otherworld to this world, from
> blindness to bright-eyes . . . from spinning to weaving, from im-
> penetrable erratic compulsion to the practical intellect's foresighted
> protective measures in regard to necessity, which measures them-
> selves become another kind of necessity. This psychological process
> I would define as normalization and I would consider Athene to
> be the archetypal person within the fantasy of normality. When
> psychology speaks in terms of norms, when it attempts to nor-
> malize, when it represents the point of view of the cultural canon
> and gives wise counsel from the practical understanding—pro-
> tective, hygienic, politic, sensible—then psychology is enacting
> Athene. (Hillman 1980, 27)

Hillman's commentary notwithstanding, to effect a reconciliation between
Zeus and the Erinyes is not to represent "the point of view of the cultural
canon" but is at once to acknowledge and to *change* the cultural canon, to
alter its chemistry. The prevailing cultural canon in the age of Aischylos
would have eliminated the Erinyes altogether; Athene placed that ancient
chthonian power at the very center of her sanctuary on the Akropolis. As
David Miller puts it,

> Athena knows it would be unrealistic in an apollonian age—an age
> of increasing complexity in war and political life, an age of rapid
> urbanization and technology, an age of specialized knowledge and
> expertise, and an age of heightened philosophical self-conscious-
> ness and agonizing reflectivity—it would be unrealistic in such an
> age not to acknowledge Apollo, for the age is what Apollo is. Yet
> she makes a place for the Furies—the guardians of close family ties
> among blood relatives, the chthonic deities of the ecological bal-
> ance in nature, the upholders of femininity. . . . Athena acknowledges
> in the Furies the deep rootedness of the origin and fate of an
> apollonian people. (D. Miller 1981, 52)

This, in fact, is a perfect image for what was historically true of Greek religion: the Olympian became the "official" religion of the aristocracy, while the old order was still revered among the common people—and more often than not, covertly by the aristocrats as well. So in this sense, too, Athene was symbolically a political cross-dresser; she possessed the internal psychological "garments" which allowed her to act and to participate in the power of the patriarchy without dishonoring her chthonian, matriarchal roots. This, in turn, allowed her to fulfill her goal of good for the people.

THE NATURE AND RANGE OF ATHENE'S CREATIVITY

Perhaps the most important aspect of the goddess in her embodiment of the creative is her sheer inventiveness; she refuses to be limited by the givens of a situation and can conceptualize a new thing out of an old or even out of a completely blank field. This requires a willingness to step outside the collective, sometimes even to go against it, since the collective requires considerable stasis in order to maintain its security. To the collective, as to individuals, change—even beneficial change—can be seen as a threat.

Part of Athene's inventiveness is her ability to call on different facets of the self to meet the demands of the occasion, and this ability alone bespeaks a high degree both of psychological creativity and of personal integrity: only when we are sure enough of our essential identity can we cause or risk a temporary shift in its outward expression.

Athene's creativity is often pragmatic and utilitarian, as in the invention of the bridle, the ox-yoke, the ship. But even these do not lack felicity, which has its own kind of aesthetic. Perhaps we more readily find beauty expressed in the creation of the flute, weaving, or pottery. From the range of inventions with which Athene is credited, we may infer that she is not afraid of hard work—she was, after all, called *Ergane* (Worker), and Harrison suggests this was probably a reference to work "in the Hesiodic sense, of tilth rather than of weaving and handicraft" (Harrison 1991, 519)—in other words, to the plain, hard, unglamorous work of farming. This connection may, in fact, predate Hesiod's time, since scholars are now beginning to believe that the "wealth" of Mycenae and the treasures over which the *potnia* presided derived from its rich fields.

Athene's association with the creative dates to her earliest origins: the creative would naturally be part of her legacy from the Great Mother. As patroness of the utilitarian and decorative arts, Athene was credited with the invention of the ship,[4] the plough, the trumpet, potterymaking,[5] wool-working (weaving), the bridle and ox-yoke, all mechanical arts, the science of number, and the *aulos*, a double flute made of stag bones.[6]

These are not the inventions of a warmonger; they argue Athene's birth in a civilization whose harmony and cultural achievements could flourish only in peace and freedom of time and space for explorative, innovative vision. Of Athene these creative achievements tell us again that human wellbeing and advancement were among her preoccupations.

In summary, all of Athene's qualities bespeak a superb psychological balance. It is as though she were an extraordinary walker perpetually keeping sure footing at the always shifting juncture where the opposites meet. As such, she is an archetypal embodiment not of the normative but of the transcendent function, that "third thing" which arises out of the conflict between opposites and which at once contains the opposites and transcends them.

If Athene contains and unifies the opposites, and if her personality was shaped by Aidos, goddess not of "shame," as we have seen, but of Reverence and self-respect, would not the opposite of Aidos necessarily be present? And what would be the opposite of Aidos/*aidos*? Logically, the direct opposite would be "that which is not *aidos*," the absence of reverence.[7] Applying Democritus' view, the opposite of *aidos* would be the absence of reverence for one's self; extreme and complete absence of self-reverence would be the kind of deep shame described in much of the literature cited in the first chapter: the sense of one's self as a defective, loathsome being.

The image in Greek myth which, in my opinion, depicts with terrifying accuracy the hellish state of tormented shame is the Gorgon, and I am positing that image as the opposite of *aidos* and as the third archetypal figure in our triad. I do so knowing that it wrenches somewhat the old Greek constructs, but am nonetheless encouraged to pursue the idea because of its persuasive psychological aptness and because the Gorgon image is perhaps the most striking and mysterious one connected with Athene.[8]

ATHENE AND THE GORGON

Most of us are reasonably familiar with both the story and the image of the Gorgon. In the standard version of the tale, the Gorgons were three sisters, Sthenno (Strong One), Euryale (Wide-leaping), and Medousa

58

(Queen), who happened to be the only mortal member of the trio. They lived, said Hesiod, "beyond the stream/of famous Ocean, on the edge near Night" (Hesiod 1973, 274-5; Wender trans.). To the Greeks, that meant northwest Africa near the range of the Atlas mountains in present-day Morocco (Rose 1991, 105), an area which the early Greeks referred to as Libya.[9]

Medousa, we all know, was pursued and killed by the hero Perseus, but there are several versions of how she became the object of his pursuit. In one version, Perseus is given the task by his new stepfather, who wanted him out of the way. But probably the best known version is that Medousa dishonored Athene's temple by lying there with Poseidon,[10] a violation for which Athene (perhaps out of a sense of *aidos*, since the desecration of a temple was a punishable impiety) changed the once beautiful woman into a monster. From that point forward, any man who looked upon her face was changed to stone—presumably the reason Perseus sought her out, since no other motive is provided in this version. In another somewhat less mythical and probably less elderly version related by Pausanias, Medousa, as queen and therefore commander of Libyan troops, fell into battle with Perseus and his small army from the Peloponnesos. In a less than heroic action, the hero sneaked up on Medousa during the night and murdered her, but was so struck by her beauty that he removed her head to display back home.

In the most popular version, there are no doubts about Athene's interventions in behalf of Perseus. She advises him, lends him her shield to use as a mirror so he can see his quarry without risking petrifaction, and even guides his hand as he delivers the killing blow with a sickle. After Perseus has slain the Gorgon, escaped from her pursuing sisters, and lived through a number of other adventures, he offers the Gorgon head to Athene, who affixes it to her shield (or, variously, to her breastplate or *aegis*).[11] In yet another variation, Athene flays Medousa and wears her entire skin as her *aegis*. In some versions, she retains two vials of the Gorgon's blood and gives them to Asklepios. With the blood from Medousa's left side, he could raise the dead; with the blood from the right side, he could cause death.

The ritual mask associated with this tale, the *gorgoneion*, was essentially a leonine form which probably found its way into the Bronze Age Mycenaean culture through Asian influences. (Both the Minoans and the Mycenaeans were fond of the exotic, and lions were not native to Greece.) It is among the "earliest masked representations of daimons in Greek mythology and art" (Napier 1986, 53), and is the only mask form in Greek culture intended to suggest transposition to "a new and unknown . . . uncanny and unsettling world" which did not also have some admixture of "absurdity and aggressive obscenity" (Burkert 1985, 104).

Iconographically, the *gorgoneion* is characterized by a rounded face from which the eyes bulge and the tongue protrudes; tusks like those of a boar[12] thrust from a mouth which appears to be grinning, and almost always snakes are part of the image, sometimes as hair, sometimes held in the Gorgon's hands, sometimes coiled about her waist.

Harrison and some subsequent scholars hold that the *gorgoneion* came first; that first there was the mask, then the invention of the monster to account for the mask, and finally the story about the beautiful woman who was changed into a monster to provide a rationale for the creature's existence. Chances are that this progression is close to the truth, for the image the Greeks called the Gorgon is exceedingly ancient and has occurred in almost every primitive culture. There is reason to believe that the Mycenaeans borrowed the image and that later Greeks added the Medousa derivation, Athene's connections, and the presence of the hero. We know from vase paintings that what is now the common version of the tale was in place by Homer's time, and the *gorgoneion* first appears in surviving literature in the *Iliad*, on Athene's *aegis* and on Agamemnon's shield. However, it would be faulty reasoning to assume that because the Gorgon first appears in the literature and imagery of the archaic period it originated in that time. As Snell points out, the men of the *Iliad*, although they were meant to depict Mycenaean heroes, "no longer feel that they are the playthings of irrational forces; they acknowledge their Olympian gods who constitute a well-ordered and meaningful world" (1953, 22). Men of this outlook do not conjure up creatures such as the Gorgon; if she is present in their thoughts, it is because their thoughts are reaching back into a past in which "magic and sorcery held the field" (op. cit.). Moreover, we have virtually no information about the four centuries which intervened between the Homeric days and the Mycenaean, so we cannot know what the imagination of the Dark Age may have produced in the way of daimonic images, or what it held on to from the Mycenaean culture. Anthropologist Thalia Howe suggests that the formulation of the traditional image, although not appearing until early in the seventh century, took a few centuries to develop (Howe 1954, 213). Dodds (1951, 12) comments on the "high antiquity of the adjective *daemonios*," an adjective which certainly applied to the Gorgon.

Some scholars, however, assert that the myth around the image "scarcely appears before the second half of the 7th century, when it suddenly arises simultaneously throughout Greece" (Howe 1954, 219). It emerged, then, on the heels of the full-blown Olympian patriarchy, apparently incorporating Mycenaean elements. The name Perseus (etymologically, "the Cutter") seems to have come out of the Bronze Age, and Perseus is generally held to have been a Mycenaean, at one time king of Argos (variously, Tiryns).[13] There is also a pre-Olympian cast to the story in its magical and nonrational elements. Additionally, there is the fact that Perseus slays the Gorgon not with his sword (which he has with him in the vase paintings) but with a sickle. Connected with agriculture, the presence of the sickle may be a remnant of chthonic antiquity.[14]

I have argued at some length the pre-patriarchal dating of the Gorgon in order to establish its likely coexistence with the pre-patriarchal Athene and with a culture in which *aidos* still carried its connotations of encounters with the numinous, the uncanny. The pre-patriarchal Athene, not so incidentally, is linked with the uncanny and the magical—all those dark, chthonic, and "disorderly" elements abandoned by the archaic and classical Greeks, who assigned supreme value to reason and order—in her invention of divinatory dice and, as we know from iconography, with the Harpies and Sirens.

It is the *function* of the *gorgoneion*, however, which most concerns us here. Its primary function, according to Harrison, "is permanently to 'make an ugly face,' *at* you if you are doing wrong . . . *for* you if you are doing right" (Harrison 1991, 187). Thus it had both an apotropaic and an aggressive function; it was meant not only to ward off evil but to lend its wearer the power of terrorizing, even petrifying, the enemy. It can be both prophylactic, protecting the wearer, and destructive to the foe. Part of the terror it evoked, then, had to do with death, with the dissolution of existence.

To my knowledge, no one has observed the very direct and immediate link between death and the rictus and protruding tongue of the Gorgon mask. Facial muscles after death rigidify until the mouth is opened as in a grin, and the tongue extends. This alone is enough to account for the pancultural appearance of the "death bogey" and to be the basis of the Gorgon's archetypal nature.

Apparently, it was the Gorgon's eyes which were death-dealing. Homer describes her as "fire-eyed" (*Iliad* 11, 36; Fitzgerald trans.)—or, in the Fagles translation (line 40) as having "burning eyes," a word which in the Greek derived from a Sanskrit root referring to sharp sight. (It is the same word used to describe the quality of Athene's eyes; see Appendix.) It seems that the word δερκεσθαι is intended to denote the force of energy coming through the eyes, an energy which is merely acute in Athene's gaze but in the Gorgon's is lethal. As Harrison says, "The Gorgon was regarded as a sort of incarnate Evil Eye. The monster was tricked out with cruel tusks and snakes, but it slew by the eye, it fascinated" (Harrison 1991, 196). A widespread folk belief of great antiquity, the Evil Eye in the Western culture "has been attributed to the ancient Greek theory of visual perception where the eyes were thought to emanate rays that struck objects and people with sufficient power to produce physical harm or even death" (Coss 1991, 182). However, one can reasonably speculate that this idea needed no "theory of visual perception" but was a result of aggregated experiences of the affective power of the gaze—a power to which animals as well as humans react.

One final point about the Gorgon before moving into the crux of all this. Beginning with Freud, there have been several attempts to link the image of the Gorgon with the female genitalia and thus with fears of castration. Interestingly, *aidos*, too, has a connection with the genitals: "The powerful person . . . is *Aidoios. Aidoia* connotes the genital organs" (Schneider 1992, 111). While there is a useful, if rather obvious and fundamental, avenue to track here in linking Gorgon-shame-genitals, another avenue offers much richer promise. For the Greeks the head, not the genitals, was the source of the life-seed by which procreation took place. The head was held to be the seat of life, synonymous with the person, the supremely honored part of the body, co-extensive with the person's *psyche* (almost, but not quite, what we mean by "soul"). Moreover, it was the male alone who contained the psyche, which would be passed on only to his male children; the female contributed only the matter which housed the psyche (Onians 1991, 95*ff*). So potent was the head as the true progenitor that the beard was regarded as evidence of male fertility, and in one version of Athene's birth she emerges not from Zeus' forehead but from his chin (ibid., 233). The Greek infinitive for "to kill" was "to decapitate," and heads were often kept, sometimes on display on houses, for their prophetic as well as their prophylactic or apotropaic powers.

In cultural perspective, the elements of the Medousa story are somewhat less bizarre and even more meaningful. For Perseus to have used a sickle, with its evocation of farming, suggests that the head as "seed" or "fruit" was not simply separated from the body but was *harvested*; for Athene to have retained and worn the head was to have reclaimed and deployed the life-seed of a highly potent form of the primordial and the chthonic. In an act not unlike that of Prometheus' stealing of the Olympian fire, Perseus released, or stole back, the power of the fire-eyed, fiercely apotropaic, chthonic feminine. The act may be the only tacit admission in Greek myth that a mortal woman, as Medousa was, is more than matter and that the psyche does not reside exclusively in the male head. It runs counter to the beliefs of the archaic period, which may be when the story was invented, and counter to the belief which runs right up through Aristotle and beyond, into the early Church, that women have no souls.

Several names can be given to this image. Neumann might have referred to it as the Terrible Mother, the "overwhelming character of the Great Mother" (Neumann 1970, 215). Woodward (1937) says that she "embodies the great Nature Spirit of primitive belief" (39); Harrison that she is the "ugly bogey-, Erinyes-side of the Great Mother . . . a potent goddess, not as in later days a monster to be slain by heroes," and with her usual pungency adds that the great divinities of the chthonian religion, in which awe, dread, and mystery were central, became the "bogeys" of the Olympian, in which law and order were central, dread and mystery anathema (Harrison 1991, 194).

From any point of view, the Gorgon, with her uncanny, unmanageable, dark, potentially death-dealing, terror-inspiring energies, is an entity who points straight into what Paul Ricoeur has called the taboo area of the sacred. Hers is an archetypal image whose effects offer compelling parallels with the effects of deep shame: the sense of paralysis (petrifaction); the sense of exposure, of being *seen* in a devastating way (the gaze of the Evil Eye); the terror of extinction; the psyche (head) as the seat of energy; the involvement of death. In this perspective, the Gorgon could be called the archetypal image of shame and dread, and the opposite of *aidos*. It is to these issues that we turn in the next chapter.

63

NOTES TO CHAPTER TWO

1. Arachne is changed into a spider by Athene when she audaciously challenges the goddess to a weaving contest. Athene's reaction was more benign when she caught Aphrodite working at a loom—she only complained that her territory was being invaded and threatened to abandon weaving altogether. When Aphrodite apologized, she withdrew the threat.

2. The Erichthonios myth is readily available and need not be reiterated here. Erichthonios was a snake god with origins in the Minoan-Mycenaean religion; his cult was carried through to survival in the classical period. As Nilsson comments, "Erichthonios came to be regarded as a mythical ancestor and king of Athens in olden times, but his real nature was not quite forgotten. Herodotus says that he was called 'the earth born', and Euripides that he rose from the earth . . . [He] is firmly bound up with the oldest cults of the Acropolis. He shared a temple with Athena . . . situated in the ruins of the Mycenaean palace on the Acropolis" (Nilsson 1949, 562-3). In this same passage, Nilsson identifies Erichthonios as "the Divine Child," which is called Ploutos at Eleusis, "the new-born spirit of vegetation and the crops, which is given over to others to rear," an idea, he says, which "belonged to the religion of the Minoan people" (ibid., 572). In this way, the Erichthonios myth joins with others, e.g., that Athene was one of Persephone's companions when she was snatched by Hades, that early sacrifices to Athene were originally done not with fire and animals—that came in with the Olympian religion—but with barley, the grain so closely associated with Demeter and the Eleusinian mysteries; joins with others to imply, however covertly, some very early kinship between Athene and Demeter.

3. Cross-dressing in itself bespeaks Athene's antiquity, for no female Hellene from the Dark Ages on was allowed to join in the affairs of men, in politics, war, the hunt, even in debate or intellectual exchange. Perhaps we need only to know that Athenian wives were not even allowed to leave their houses except on rare occasions such as the women's festivals; when they did leave, they were kept under close surveillance. In the city-state which established the world's first democracy, women had the same status as slaves, which is to say they could not own property, nor could they vote. Like slaves, they did not have the status of citizen. It is much easier to see the self-assured, exuberant Athene emerging from the Minoan culture, in which women drove chariots, joined in the hunt, held religious and political office, probably inherited property through the mother, and enjoyed many if not all of the social prerogatives of the male.

4. A distinctly Minoan tie, since the Minoans were renowned navigators; the Mycenaeans were not, although eventually they learned how to fill Minoan shoes.

5. Again, probably a relic of the Minoan culture. The Minoans are often credited with having developed the first hand-turned wheel in the Aegean, ca. 2500.

6. This also hints at Athene's ties with the old chthonic order. The *aulos*, says Georgiades, "is the instrument of exaltation and ecstasy, the instrument of the dithyramb," unlike the lyre, invented by Hermes, which is the "instrument of Homer, of the *epos*, of the serene contemplation of the universe . . . The lyre is the instrument of Apollo, the *aulos* that of the Dionysiac festivals" (Georgiades n.d., 46-7). Some sources indicate that Athene invented the instrument to preserve the sounds of Euryales' grief when her sister Medousa was killed.

7. The Greeks, in particular the archaic Greeks, had another way of looking at this. If one's sense of *aidos* (here, the respect due one) was violated, the response to that sense of violation was the emotion of *nemesis*, often defined as "righteous indignation." Thus if A fails to honor B, B prevails upon A's sense of *aidos*, respect for B's honors. If this is to no avail, B then experiences *nemesis*. This is a simple situation which might have occurred in Homer's time, one which had an entirely social context, since by then the concept of *aidos* has been severed from its original religious context. I believe it is valid to say that before the affect of righteous indignation erupted, B's first affect would have been one of shame, *aischyne*, in the sense that we commonly feel shame today. These combined affects can escalate from "righteous indignation" to rage, as they did in Akhilleus after Agamemnon took Briseus from him—as they did, in fact, after Zeus raped Nemesis. Burkert describes Nemesis at that point as "clearly a double of the raging Demeter Erinys" (Burkert 1985, 185).

8. But it is not the only image of the uncanny, the daimonic, and the mysterious. One of Athene's inventions was divinatory dice fashioned from knuckle bones, an invention which links her with the Daktyloi, phallic daimones associated with Kybele, the Great Mother. The Daktyloi first bore the label of smith, or metalworker, now a craft but back then held to be a form of magic. Insofar as they are associated with Kybele, they were said to be denizens of Crete. Athene's ties to smithing are also seen in a variant story of her parentage, in which Brontes the Kyklops is her father. The Kyklopes were smiths, phallic primordial beings, and were said to have taken charge of the young Athene's education. It is not unreasonable to suspect the Athene-Daktyloi-Kyklops-smithing association to have been the source of later stories relating Athene to Hephaistos.

Other apparent connections to the daimonic chthonian include those to the Harpies, winged women-demons who both snatch souls away to death and bring things to life and who are involved with the winds, sometimes riding, sometimes controlling them. Three kinds of images tie Athene to the Harpies: wings (she is sometimes portrayed as winged and sometimes appears accompanied by an odd little bird-woman); winds (there was an Athene of the Winds, and stories of her control of the wind); and horses (as Athene Hippia, horse goddess, she provokes associations with the Harpy mother of the horses of Akhilleus, with Demeter, and with Medousa, occasionally depicted as half horse, half woman).

9. The Greeks often ascribed exotic locations to the more monstrous figures in their myths, perhaps because they often borrowed such figures from other cultures, in particular those of Egypt and Asia Minor. Since these figures were almost always female, such distancing could be seen as symptomatic of the patriarchy's fear and repression of the feminine. Howe makes this point: "The memory of the sorceress type remained vital and integral to [the Greek] culture, while the actual figures and their dominant social role had virtually disappeared. . . . But in the case where there still remains hearsay knowledge of such figures, the primitive mind may argue that such things continue to exist, but not locally—only further off, among foreign peoples. Hence we may say that where chronological accuracy does not yet appear, there may arise a *substitution* of space for time. This . . . probably in part explains why it is that so many of the protagonists are exotic and the liveliest events seem to be taking place in the present yet in distant realms . . . " (Howe 1969, 162).

According to one myth, Athene was sent to Libya by Zeus to be reared and tutored. If, as some scholars have contended, it was the Libyans who settled Crete and developed the civilization known as the Minoan, a little more light is shed on the reasons for several associations of Athene with Libya. Some say that Athene was born at Lake Tritonis, the daughter of the river god Triton and sister of Pallas, whom she accidentally killed and whose name she then added to her own.

10. Some stories declare Poseidon to have been the father both of Athene and of Medousa, and there is considerable material to give credence to this paternity of Athene—e.g., that Poseidon was originally chthonic and Mycenaean, not a god of the sea but of earthquakes and underground streams; and the association of both deities with water and horses.

11. Among scholars there seems not to be absolute agreement about the nature of the *aegis*, except that it was made of the skin of a goat (the Greek word for goat is *aix*, from which *aegis* is derived). Burkert (1985) speaks of it as a pectoral, which is to say it was worn on the chest (a breastplate), as do Gilbert Murray (1955) and Harrison (1963). Graves (1959) cites Herodotus: "Athene's garments and *aegis* were borrowed by the Greeks from the Libyan women, who are dressed in exactly the same way, except that their garments are fringed with thongs, not serpents." He goes on to posit that the *aegis* was a "goat-skin chastity tunic worn by Libyan girls . . . hence the prophylactic Gorgon mask set above it and the serpent concealed in [a] leather pouch" (ibid., 47), or that it was a "magical goat-skin bag containing a serpent and protected by a Gorgon mask" and that it "was Athene's long before Zeus claimed to be her father" (ibid., 44). Kerényi notes that the *gorgoneion* was worn by Athene "either as a sign on her shield or attached to her breastplate, which was her sacred goatskin named Aegis. It was even supposed that the Gorgon had been the original owner of this goatskin . . . " (Kerényi 1951, 50). Bernard Knox (1990) acknowledges the confusion and observes that at one point in the text of the *Iliad* the "aegis" appears to be a shield with "the figure of the Gorgon's head and other forms of terror" on it (623, n. 2.529). Unfortunately, Mycenaean battle gear does not provide a clue, since typically both the shield and the breastplate were made of hide (sometimes covered with bronze) and very few examples have survived. Certainly by the classical period the *aegis* seems to have been defined as a shield, judging from an Athenian cup by the Brygos Painter (the so-called "Ransom of Hector," ca. 490-480). Rose (1991), however, convinces by his simplicity. The word, he says, just means "goat-skin." In its origin "this mysterious object is nothing more than a cloak made of a goat's hide with the hair on, forming a fringe. . . . As it was of tough hide, it would serve its wearer as a defence, not only against the weather, but against an enemy's blows" (48).

12. That the tusks are always said to be those of a boar suggests an indirect link with the Mycenaean culture, in which helmets featured boar's tusks laid in a curved pattern over hide. This manner of making helmets ended with the Mycenaeans.

13. According to Pausanias, the people of Argos claimed that the Gorgon head was buried in their town.

14. Howe (1954, 216, n. 42) mentions but immediately discounts what we perhaps should not: an earlier scholar's assertion that the sickle was originally a snake motif that evolved into a weapon, along the lines of the serpent-weapon of the Babylonian caduceus.

Chapter Three

The Daemonic Sacred, Defilement, and the Gorgon

It is completely forgotten that the reason mankind believes in the "daemon" has nothing whatever to do with outside factors, but is due to simple perception of the powerful inner effect of the autonomous fragmentary systems. . . . We are still as possessed by our autonomous psychic contents as if they were gods. . . . It is not a matter of indifference whether one calls something a "mania" or a "god." To serve a mania is detestable and undignified, but to serve a god is decidedly more meaningful and more productive because it means an act of submission to a higher, spiritual being.

— C. G. Jung, in *The Secret of the Golden Flower*

Although comparatively few publications have focused on shame, the issue is implicit in any discussion of the narcissistic wound, whether that wound is called a feeling of being intrinsically unloveable, the wounded child complex, object relations failures, and so forth. The term "shame" is rarely used; more typically we see references to distress, anxiety, fragmentation, disintegration. Each of these terms, while it may indeed denote a discrete psychological condition, can also be understood to imply the presence of shame, lurking in the affective shadows cast by its crisp denotative outline. Perhaps clinical diction has, on the whole, found the little monosyllable, worn down by centuries of being handed around in common parlance ("Shame on you!"), unworthy of admission to diagnostic vocabulary, no longer large enough to convey the soul-killing effects of such a disintegrative experience.

This failure of nomenclature, the apparent uncertainty about how to admit shame *per se* to the diagnostic canon, and what look like

67

ambiguities in identifying the etiology of shame and in developing a taxonomy for it, all may result from reluctance to probe deeply enough into the issue. Beneath the explications of shame discussed in received theory, there is *for some of us* another deeper explication which can extend, not repudiate, what is already understood by clinicians. That deeper—probably *deepest*—layer takes us into the religious dimension, and it is there where we may find another way, still holding psychology by one hand, to grasp the nature of ontic shame.

We shall be working with several terms which ordinarily appear in religious studies and in philosophical anthropology, among them: the numinous, the sacred, defilement, dread. Together they are the pillars of my thesis:

> In some shamecarriers, at some time before the ego is formed, the infant psyche encounters the daemonic aspect of the sacred, the dark side of the numen; this encounter imprints the infant's archaic psyche with a sense not of "shame" but of its own defilement and consequent feeling of dread which, unless mitigated by a holding environment created by an empathic mother, becomes pervasive and chronic.

We shall look at the elements of that statement one by one, setting them in the context of received psychological theory.

THE CAPACITIES OF THE INFANT PSYCHE

Let's start with the idea that the pre-ego psyche can "encounter." Implicit in that idea is the premise that the infant is a "self" of sufficient formation to experience and to retain experience, however unconsciously. And implicit in that premise is the question, how early in life can this happen?

There is much we still do not know about the fetal and infant brain, still less about the infant psyche. Much of what we do know has been discovered only in the last decade or two and is radically altering our perceptions—altering them, in fact, to the point of validating thought heretofore viewed by science as "mystical" at best, preposterous at worst. Here are some of the salient facts, for which I have relied on Richard M. Restak (1986):

> The synapses have begun to form by about the second month of gestation; by birth the process is well advanced.

Learning occurs in the subcortical centers of the brain, which is almost
identical to that of the "lower" animals, as well as in the cerebral hemisphere; the neural plate develops about three to four weeks after
conception, and from it "arise the most special parts of a human being:
dreams, illusions, griefs, tenderness, lust."

The fetus, by the fifteenth week, has sixteen movements, including the
startle reaction.

At thirteen weeks the fetus begins sucking its thumb.

Tests and experiments have shown that the fetus can experience pleasure
and displeasure.

We have assumed, on the basis of facial expressions, that certain affects are
not present in infants, but there is now evidence that a range of affects,
including fear and sadness, is present but their components may not be
organized sufficiently to manifest in a way recognized by adults. Restak
has seen sadness in an abused three-month-old, and states that babies
may *feel* but not be able to manifest.

These and similar findings argue the presence of prenatal affective capacities,
including the capacity to experience fear, displeasure, apprehension, the need
for comfort and security. As Aldo Carotenuto writes,

> Recent studies on prenatal life have revealed that there can be envi-
> ronmental influences on the psychic life of the unborn child.
> According to some experts, this influence consists not only of the
> psychological effect on the future personality of the child in early
> infancy which the mother's emotional state can have—as a result
> of a whole network of relationships affecting the woman—but also
> the mother's imagining of the child even before it is born.
> (Carotenuto 1992, 102)

Heinz Kohut, although not commenting on prenatal influences, answers
in the affirmative his question of whether it is possible to "substantiate a
hypothesis of the presence of a rudimentary self in infancy." He stresses
that "the human environment reacts to even the smallest baby as if it had
already formed a self"—that from the beginning the infant is "fused via
mutual empathy with an environment that does experience him as already
possessing a self." If these concepts are valid, he asks, "may we then not

speak of a self *in statu nascendi* even at a time when the infant in isolation—a psychological artifact—can be looked upon only as a biological unit?" (Kohut 1977, 98-100)

Others extend Kohut's thought to assert that being treated as a self registers prenatally. On the mother's capacity for containing the unborn child's primary emotions (Bion's "reverie"), Carotenuto comments, "This capacity of reverie also functions during the period of gestation, in the period of preparation. In this emotional state, for reasons still unknown, the sensation of existence because someone considers that existence, even expecting it and determining it through that desire, is transmitted to the fetus" (Carotenuto 1992, 102). D. W. Winnicott writes that "there is nothing to be gained by wrangling over the date at which . . . human nature itself starts. The only certain date is that of conception. The date of birth is obviously notable, but much has happened before . . . " (Winnicott 1988, 29).

> An ability on the part of the baby before birth to retain body memories is something which must be allowed for, since there is a certain amount of evidence that from a date prior to birth nothing that a human being experiences is lost. (Ibid., 126-7)

> The point of view I am putting forward here is that, at full term, there is already a human being in the womb, one that is capable of having experiences and of accumulating body memories and even of organizing defensive measures to deal with traumata. . . . (Ibid., 143)

Whatever we call this—a "self" or a "self *in statu nascendi*" or an "individuality"—the evidence argues that before the ego is formed there is (let us call it) a fairly complex "receiving center," or what Winnicott calls a "central organisation" (ibid., 126), and that this center is present before birth.

There is one more point to be made in connection with the pre-ego psyche. According to Restak, the development of the neural plate, the formation of the synapses, and the occurrence of learning in the subcortical brain centers make up the first formation of the primitive or archaic brain. The archaic brain is overshadowed, as we develop, by the more complex cerebral hemisphere but it does not disappear with maturity psychologically any more than it does physically. It continues to respond, imagine, and work even in the most conscious, intelligent, and sophisticated of us; it is the seat of the archaic psyche which keeps us kin to other animals and to the world of the instincts. It also serves as the archive of our kinship to primitive man. In fact, according to some scientists, we are each examples of ontogeny recapitulating philogeny, which is to say that individual development recapitulates the development (evolution) of the race: we begin as a primitive, archaic being and (one hopes) develop beyond that. But always *around* that. This is so even from a purely physiological standpoint; we have the evolution in miniature in the physical development of the brain: as the brain develops the final neurons make their way to the surface by *passing through* the area occupied by all the earlier neurons.

And so we can only conclude that there is indeed a prenatal psychic center which is archaic (but is also the ego-self *in potentia*), vulnerable to stimulation, both extra- and intrapsychically, capable of affective response and of organizing defenses. This center, by whatever name, is undoubtedly the stem of the personality and is probably an early indication of the presence of what Jung named the self. I believe it is safe to say that it is also (perhaps *therefore*) the seat of what Neumann (1990) calls "'mythological apperception,' which is still unaccompanied by an ego-consciousness" (86), therefore of the archetypal psyche or collective unconscious, and probably of what the philosophers call innate or *a priori* knowledge.

> The mythological theory of foreknowledge . . . explains the view that all knowing is "memory." Man's task in the world is to remember with his conscious mind what was knowledge before the advent of consciousness. . . . It is the same conception as Plato's philosophical doctrine of the prenatal vision of ideas and their remembrance. The original knowledge of one who is still enfolded in the perfect state is very evident in the psychology of the child. . . . In the child the great images and archetypes of the collective unconscious are living reality, and very close to him. . . . It is transpersonal experience not personally acquired, a possession acquired from "over there." Such knowledge is rightly regarded as ancestral knowledge. . . . Jung therefore defines the transpersonal—or the archetypes and instincts of the collective unconscious—as "the deposit of ancestral experience." (Neumann 1970, 23)

THE DAEMONIC ASPECT OF THE SACRED

With the second element of the thesis, the daemonic area of the sacred, we enter the field of an essential mystery, of something which can be

71

experienced but cannot be fully cognized, demonstrated, or proved. Nonetheless, an experience which we ourselves can have, about which we can read in mythology, anthropology, religious studies, and the nature of which can be intuited from the artifacts of antiquity, need not be empirically demonstrable or scientifically measurable in order to be validated—just as dreams cannot (to date) be empirically confirmed but are *known*. (A chaos physicist told me once that artificial stimulation of the limbic brain consistently induces archetypal images. Ever since then I have had a fantasy that one day we will be able to videotape our dreams.)

To characterize an aspect of the sacred as daemonic inevitably suggests a question which simply cannot be answered, the question of the nature of the divine. Of what we cannot know, we cannot speak—or, as Wittgenstein put it, "what we cannot talk about we must pass over in silence" (Wittgenstein 1961, 3), a viewpoint steadfastly ignored by generations of very talkative theologians. The idea that there is an area of the sacred which is daemonic is almost completely inadmissible in the Judaeo-Christian tradition, which all the while insisting that god is omnipresent, omniscient, the center and circumference, etc., paradoxically (not to say illogically) also insists that god is love and is All Good. (The latter, by the way, is a trace element of the classical Greek outlook in which the norms of the state were equated with the nature of the divine; if the divine was good, then the laws of the state represented the good, making a single transgression at once illegal and impious.) Evil, therefore, is "not-god," and must be held either (a) not to be real (thus the church's tenacity in the idea that evil is the absence of good, from which one can only draw the conclusion that there is, after all, some place where god does not exist); or (b) located in the human, a perspective which drives a new wedge between god and god's creation, tends to deny the imprint of divinity in the human being, intensifies our sense of alienation and defilement, and generally accounts for a whole mess of havoc in our psychology. Either way, god is perceptually "split," evil is eventually hypostatized as the Devil, and the church has unwittingly either recognized or created a shadow side of god, all the while denying that it exists.

Other religions have done a better job of leaving the divine intact, sometimes simply by not trying to introduce the category of the Moral into the category of the Holy. But almost every religion except Protestant Christianity has retained some degree of official recognition that what is sacred is also, somewhere, taboo, and that this area may be approached only by those who are ritually prepared, and then only with the greatest *aidos*. Probably the single remaining trace of this attitude in organized Christianity is in the Catholic church, where only the priest is qualified to handle the Host. No more!

However, our purpose here is not to ignore Wittgenstein by trying to speak of the unspeakable, but to speak of *perceptions* and *experiences*, which are both knowable and speakable. First, then, what do we mean by the "daemonic?"

Almost without exception the term is used today as synonymous with "satanic" or "evil"—a meaning it acquired with Xenocrates, a philosopher contemporary with Aristotle, i.e., of the Hellenistic period. It is used here, however, in its earliest sense, to mean a potency: the aspect of the divine which cannot be anthropomorphized (Harrison 1991, 587). Similarly, Ricoeur states that the expression *daimon* "represents the divine as close to undifferentiated power; and so it provides an apt designation for the sudden, irrational, invincible apparition of the divine in the emotional and volitional life of man" (Ricoeur 1967, 215-6). Jung's understanding would seem to agree with Harrison's and Ricoeur's; he writes of the "primitive energetic notion of god, in which the impelling *dynamis* has not crystallized into the abstract idea of god" (1976, 316). Jung's experience of the Holy apparently centered on the daimonic aspect; Edinger cites an interview with Jung only days before his death in 1961 in which he was asked about his understanding of god:

> He replied in these words: "To this day god is the name by which I designate all things which cross my willful path violently and recklessly, all things which upset my subjective views, plans and intentions and change the course of my life for better or worse." (Edinger 1974, 101)

Burkert comes close to making the same distinction between the *dynamis* and the abstraction: "Speaking of *theos* or *theoi* [god or gods], one posits an absolute and insurmountable point of reference for everything that has impact, validity, and permanence, while indistinct and impenetrable influences which often affect man directly can be called *daimon*" (Burkert 1985, 272).

If something can become a point of reference, it can be understood in terms of human categories, which is to say it can be anthropomorphized, personified, and personalized. That which cannot be made an absolute point of reference and is not accessible to human categories, which remains quintessentially mystery, is "indistinct and impenetrable" and cannot be cast in the human image. It is the latter which is the daemonic aspect of the sacred. I use the word "aspect" despite my belief that we need to consider the distinct possibility that the daemonic, the ineffable mysterious, may be the *entire reality* of the divine. Those relatively few of us who hold this view stand with the early Hebrews, for whom there was only one god,

> and if there was good and evil in the world, if man suffered tragedy as well as received blessings, if human beings succumbed to dark moods and evil passions, all these things must originate with Yahweh. . . . It would be easy to dismiss the Old Testament image of god as primitive. . . . Yet, for all of its primitive quality there is a basic integrity to the image of god that we find in pre-exilic biblical literature. We may be bothered by the idea that Yahweh sends good as well as evil, but it nevertheless presents us with a bold and un-flinching monotheism. The ancient Hebrews, with their instinctive religious genius, were grasping the idea that there was one underlying reality to all phenomena, and if this meant that evil, as well as good, came from Yahweh, then this was a conclusion to be faced fearlessly. (Sanford 1981, 27)

Remnants of this view can be found here and there in Christian mysticism, most notably in Boehme, who equates the wrath of god with Hell, implying the original unity of god as the supreme *coincidentia oppositorum*.

It was the daemonic aspect which Western civilization as a whole split away from the *imago Dei*, preferring either to ignore the question altogether or to concoct a god who is largely comprehensible, entirely benevolent, mostly dependable, sometimes even rather simpleminded, a cozy father figure, a sort of Ronald Reagan in the ether. Essentially, we have created the image of a god in which the orderly, the rational, and the just are valued—a valuation based primarily on the so-called masculine principle and on a patriarchal cosmogony. It is to this version of god that the Westerner usually prays, the underlying premise being that rational speech will produce the rational (desired) effect in a rational and benevolent being. Similarly, the Greeks in the late periods fashioned the concept of *do ut des*, "I give so that you will give," which "allowed the worshipper to feel that he had established an ordered, two-sided relation with the god" (Parker 1989, 259).

We shudder and flee from the idea that the divine comprises, in the words of Gilbert Murray, "'Things which Are,' things utterly non-human and non-moral which bring man bliss or tear his life to shreds without a break in their own serenity"—a passage cited by Harrison (1991), who goes on to say of the Greeks what could equally well be said of the contemporary Westerner: "It is these real gods, this life itself, that the Greeks, like most men, were inwardly afraid to recognize and face, afraid even to worship" (ibid., 657). Because this divine is impenetrable and can tear human life to shreds, we experience it as chaotic, or potentially so; it is infinite and incomprehensible and cannot fit into our finite human constructs and categories. Because it is impersonal and cannot be delimited through anthropomorphizing as a benevolent cosmic parent concerned with our wellbeing, we experience it as threatening, hostile, potentially evil. We label it as daemonic in the ordinary sense and devalue it in our culture since it is beyond control, bargaining, appeasement. In a culture such as ours, in which emphasis is placed on power and the profitable management of nature, the "irrational," uncontrollable aspect of the sacred is equated with evil. Since it is anathema to the patriarchal dream of steady, chartable "progress," it is also linked with what is not-masculine, therefore with the feminine. In this curious circuitry, the feminine and evil become linked: Eve and the serpent.

Rudolf Otto holds that the perception of the daemonic sacred is characteristic of primitive man and that as man evolved in consciousness and civilization, the perception of "the 'god'" as daemonic gradually grew to "more and more lofty manifestations" (1958, 73). He seems almost to be arguing that the evolution of our species became a total transformation in which the primitive psyche was altered so substantially as to become a psyche of another order. Implicit in his statement is the belief that only primitive man experiences god as daemonic, when in fact we know that profound contemporary experience of the *mysterium* does include the *tremendum* as well as the *fascinans* and the

75

augustum, the central hallmarks of the Holy. We know now, through the biological sciences and through psychology, that we never entirely transcend the archaic structures of the physical brain or of the psyche. "The early stages [of individual emotional development] are never truly abandoned," said Winnicott (1988, 158). As Henri Bergson put it, the human mind works the same in "civilized" and "uncivilized" man, "but it may not be working on the same material . . . " (1954, 104).

Not to fault Otto, however. As Paul Pruyser says of him,

> He rescued the numinous from being invested only by pleasant, positive affect. The numinous mystery is, qua mystery, both a *tremendum* and a *fascinans*. It always invokes both shuddering and admiration. It attracts and repels at once. It elicits devotion and fear. It instills dread and trust. It is dangerous and comforting. It inspires awe and bliss. Moreover, Otto inferred that the aspect of the *tremendum* is more conspicuous at the beginning of religion, and that the scales are only gradually being tipped in favor of the *fascinans*. It is quite a step from awe to trust, or from a god of wrath to a god of love. The dynamic core of awe persists, no matter what else is added in later refinements. As long as the Holy remains a mystery, it is a *tremendum*. The moment it loses its mysterious features it ceases to be holy; it is then a concept or a rational insight. Power is always of its essence, for the Holy is not a concept but a symbol, charged with energy. (Pruyser 1968, 336)

Whether in the archaic or later mind, it is the daemonic sacred, the unknowable, which is the *tremendum* and which becomes the taboo area of the sacred. In Pruyser's words, "The *tremendum* consists of 'all the sources of terror,' all the threats which exist or are sensed" (ibid., 337). It becomes taboo not because it inspires terror and dread but because it is "pure" in the sense not of moral purity (a human construct) but in the sense that it is uncontaminated by, unmixed with, anything not itself. In the words of anthropologist Mary Douglas, "To be holy is to be whole, to be one; holiness is unity, integrity, perfection . . . " (Douglas 1966, 68). The Holy cannot be differentiated, broken into component parts, analyzed, dissected, understood in finite terms. *It belongs to another order*, and that inspires terror. "Ultimately, what is pure is that which is totally forbidden, that is to say, whatever living men must never come into contact with. Thus, the sacred that is perfectly pure may be altogether abominable to men, since any contact with it becomes a defilement . . . " (Vernant 1990, 137).

Taboo, writes Ricoeur, "is nothing else than this condition of objects, actions, or persons that are 'isolated' or 'forbidden' because of the danger involved in contact with them" (Ricoeur 1967, 12). He elaborates both on the nature of the taboo sacred and on the hazards of contact with it:

> It is the hierophanies, as a sphere of reality, that first engender the "ontological regime" characteristic of the defiled; the peril of the soul which defilement will later serve to symbolize is at first peril in the presence of *things* which are forbidden to profane experience and which cannot be approached without risk when one is not ritually prepared. (Ibid., 11)

> A taboo is nothing else: a punishment anticipated and forestalled emotionally in an interdiction. Thus the power of the interdict, in anticipatory fear, is a deadly power. If one goes back still further, the shadow of punishment extends over the whole region and over the very source of the interdictions, and darkens the experience of the sacred. Seen from the point of view of the vengeance and the suffering anticipated in the interdiction, the sacred reveals itself as superhuman destruction of man; the death of man is inscribed in primordial purity. And so, in fearing defilement, man fears the negativity of the transcendent; the transcendent is that before which man cannot stand; no one can see god—at least the god of taboos and interdicts—without dying. It is from this, from this wrath and this terror, this deadly power of retribution, that the sacred gets its character of separateness. It cannot be touched; for if it is touched—that is to say, violated—its death-dealing power is unleashed. (Ibid., 33)

Nietzsche anticipated Ricoeur by about half a century in this passage on shame in its original religious sense of *aidos*:

> Shame exists everywhere where there is a "mystery"; this, however, is a religious idea, which was widely extended in the older times of human civilization. Everywhere there were found bounded domains

to which access was forbidden by divine right, except under certain conditions; at first locally, as for example, certain spots that ought not to be trodden by the feet of the uninitiated, in the neighborhood of which these latter experienced horror and fear. (Nietzsche 1910, 6:99; Zimmern trans.)

This mystery "seems desecrated or in danger of desecration through us" (Nietzsche 1911, 7:232; Cohn trans.).

Certain infant psyches have "touched" the daemonic, taboo area of the sacred. They stand in relation to ego consciousness much as primitive man, encountering the same numinosity, stands in relation to modern theological constructs. Both have looked upon "the living god," the non-human "Things which Are," the *tremendum*. At this stage of psychic development, the holy is pure numen, pure energy and force and is not yet invested with rational, moral, or ethical constructs. It is not yet the god who is love.

With all these things in mind, I tried a small experiment to see if I could replicate intellectually the archaic psyche's affective experience of the encounter. Only as I was writing about it did I realize that it was also a way of retracing cognitively an experience I had several years before. Alone, I had been reading late into the night Margaret Atwood's novel *Surfacing* and was deeply engaged by the long passage in which the pregnant central character is circling around in the woods. Suddenly, I became aware of a presence behind me, perhaps no more than two feet away. I froze, unable to move, unable to continue reading but pretending to do so, my eyes still fixed on the book. Within seconds, I could feel my heart beating faster and the little hairs on the back of my neck beginning to rise. I knew that I was the subject of a visitation from a presence, a concentrated transhuman force field, and I was too awestricken to turn around. I have never been certain that this was not in part a cowardice, but I believe it was an instinctive sense of discretion—of *aidos*—as much as fear which kept me from turning. I believe it was wise not to look. While I felt the deepest awe, there was no sense of evil in the presence, only of transhuman power. My terror seemed a natural component of awe, a response to the vast unknown, the mysterium, and to my relationship to it as a "mereness" whose only majesty and dignity lay in the capacity to sit, intact, under its gaze.

In the experiment, I resolved to see if through the activity of the intellect I could arrive at the conditions which would prevail in a primitive, archaic encounter with the numinous. I began with the question, "What cognates are available independent of the constructs of history, theology, philosophy, all of culture?" The process of peeling those away as they occurred to me was interesting in itself; one by one, the thoughts which came had to be discarded because they belonged to a post-archaic system of one kind or another, and this was instructive to me about the depth to which I am buried in the collective.

Finally, I got to the bottom, or what I took to be the bottom: the first level of experience, which at once depends on the sensory and on the human capacity to perceive opposites. The primitive human, I saw, would have only those to bring to an encounter with the numen; the underlying premise would be "I am what I know; *that* is not-I and not known and therefore is the opposite of what I am." From that, the next set of postulates, based on the sensory: "I am visible, material, touchable, sensible (sensate), and living; *that* is invisible, immaterial (even though it might be momentarily resident in a material object such as a stone, a bird, a tree), untouchable, insensible, therefore not-known, unliving, and connected with another realm which I do not understand and which is death for me." From this, I concluded that to the primitive mind that which is not-known and is inimical to or inexplicable in terms of the known world would necessarily be perceived as threatening to one's existence. Moreover, this process takes place in the pre-moral, pre-theological, unconstructed world of pure nature. In that world one can feel threatened without imputing to the Other the intent of threat; it is in the nature of things to feel threatened by the Not-I, the ultimate Other, simply by virtue of its otherness, without reference to the moral-ethical categories of good and evil. (We can understand why the idea of *loving* god is not introduced until relatively late in the history of man.) And if one of the qualities of Otherness is to be "unliving"—not dead but not living as we are living—then the great threat is to our very existence; Otherness bespeaks the possibility of being made not-to-be. Surely nothing rivals that threat for its arousal of terror and dread.

Neumann's explorations suggest that this area of the daemonic, taboo sacred can be viewed as (or may be the same as) the archetypal realm, which the child experiences as "the terrible dark power of the unconscious" (Neumann 1970, 22), or as the constellation of the archetype of the Terrible Mother (Neumann 1990, 87). Jungian analysts generally would say, I believe, that regardless of the person's age, if the ego does not possess the constructs with which to encounter manifestations of the unconscious (the numinous, the *tremendum*), those manifestations will be experienced as frightening and chaotic. Jung himself at one point made a direct equation between the archaic psyche and the "whole world of the archetypes" (1966a, 77), and spoke of the "violence of all unconscious dynamism."

> In this manner the god manifests himself and in this form he must be overcome. The struggle has its parallel in Jacob's wrestling with the angel. . . . The onslaught of instinct then becomes an experience of divinity, provided that man does not succumb to it and follow it blindly, but defends his humanity against the animal nature of the divine power. It is "a fearful thing to fall into the hands of the living god" . . . for "the Lord is a consuming fire. . . . " (Jung 1967, 338)

We are reminded of Mircea Eliade's statement that "Every hierophany [manifestation of the sacred] is a kratophany, a manifestation of force" (Eliade 1960, 126).

Jung's use of the phrase "onslaught of instinct" is, if I understand it correctly, an indirect reference to his thesis that the archetypes are bipolar—are "unconscious entities having two poles, the one expressing itself in instinctual impulses and drives, the other in spiritual forms, bringing body and psyche together" (Fordham 1962, 50). It is necessarily speculative but reasonable to consider the possibility that the archetypal world *is* the daemonic sacred "sorting itself out," so to speak, into aspects of its own dynamism—in other words, that what Jungian psychology understands as discrete archetypal images are expressions of what is inherently unified and monolithic: the daimon, to which Jung gave the name the Self. It is further possible to consider that since the archetypes are bipolar, it may be that the somatic trauma experienced at birth resonates along the archetypal-psychic continuum and constellates activity at the spiritual pole. Since the birth experience is traumatic (i.e., negative), the image rising up from the activated spiritual pole would necessarily also be negative (the divine as threatening, killing). Mother's feeling and holding, if good enough, can metabolize the somatic trauma, but if her psychic state is chaotic, the spiritual trauma is not mitigated and remains imprinted in the infant psyche.

From either perspective, the infant has seen what is not meant to be seen prematurely; its psyche has encountered the taboo sacred, the *tremendum*, unsupported by ego or by culture—the categories created by language, the theological overlays of the centuries, and so forth. The baby's encounter is, in fact, vastly more naked than the encounter of primitive man, who at least has membership in a society where religious and cosmological systems are in place, systems which can address and redress the defilement resulting from transgression. For the infant, that "system" can only be the mother.

DEFILEMENT

With the idea of defilement we come to the next of the elements of the thesis, but before going into that discussion, it will probably be helpful to restate the thesis according to what has been unfolded so far.

> The pre-ego, and in all likelihood prenatal, psyche intrapsychically experiences the daemonic sacred; this, in turn, is experienced as a defilement of the self.

"Defilement" is a heavily weighted word, a repugnant word; our instinct is to shrink away from it. So we shall enter it at the least offensive door—the dictionary. Etymologically, the term comes to us out of Middle English by way of Old French, *defouler*, which meant "to trample down," which in turn came from the Latin for "to injure." From the standpoint of language, then, defilement stands in direct relation to *wound*. In terms of present-day psychological vocabulary, I think it is precisely that, the very first wounding. The "wounded child" is the *defiled* child. Witness the denotations of *defile*: (1) to make filthy or dirty (a number of my friends have had dreams in which their inner infant is a "shitty baby," a "filthy baby"); (2) to render impure, to corrupt; (3) to profane or sully; (4) to make unclean or unfit for ceremonial use, to desecrate; (5) to violate the chastity of. We are reminded of this passage from Léon Wurmser, in which he reiterates the motif of excrement, attributing contempt, however, to an outer rather than an inner aggressor:

> The loss of love in shame can be described as a radical decrease of respect for the subject as a person with his own dignity; it is a disregard

> for his having a self in its own right and with its own prestige. The
> aggression is the violent denial of any personal value in the self, the
> degradation of one's value as a person, equating him particularly with
> a debased, dirty thing—a derided and low animal or waste. The thrust
> of this aggression is to dehumanize, really to change the person into
> excrement. (Wurmser 1995, 80)

Literal physical dirtiness, in many cultures and probably among the
early Greeks, is not just a sign of being defiled but is/was taken as the defilement *per se*. Ablutions and purifications using water were, then, symbolic
but in the sense *of sacramental symbol*, in which the symbol is the thing
symbolized: the act of washing away dirt *was* the purification. This dread of
being impure ("filthy") and "rites of purification are in the background of
all our feelings and all our behavior relating to fault," believes Ricoeur (1967,
25). Ricoeur is using "fault" in its geological sense, of a cleavage or fragility
in human nature, but he might as well be using the word in Wurmser's
sense of "basic defect."

In all the denotations cited above there are religious overtones, in
the ideas of impurity, corruption, profanity, desecration, chastity. All
imply, by logical extension alone, the existence of an entity which is
pure, incorrupt and incorruptible, and holy, an entity which can therefore only be divine, and before which we are degraded and defiled
because we are seen by it and because we see it and because we are
human and "lesser than." Jean-Paul Sartre identified with precision
this wounding place:

> Our shame is not a feeling of being this or that guilty object but in
> general of being *an* object; that is, of *recognizing myself* in this de-
> graded, fixed and dependent being which I am for the Other. Shame
> is the feeling of an *original fall*. (Sartre 1956, 222)

His statement reverberates with the questions surrounding the notions of
"original sin" and the innate fallibility of man. Both notions are certainly
relevant to the present meditation (which could, in fact, even account for
their origin) but to explore that relevance in the depth it deserves would
take us too far off our main path. We turn away from this enormous subject
with these thoughts from Ricoeur:

The myth of the fall, which is the matrix of all subsequent speculations concerning the origin of evil in human freedom, is not the only myth. It does not encompass the rich mythics of chaos, of tragic blinding, or of the exiled soul. . . . What the symbolics of evil gives to thought concerns the grandeur and limitation of any ethical vision of the world. For man, as he is revealed by this symbolics, appears no less a victim than guilty. (Ricoeur 1986, xlix)

Otto might have called the sense of defilement a simple creature-consciousness, "the emotion of a creature, submerged and overwhelmed by its own nothingness in contrast to that which is supreme above all creatures. . . . All that this . . . term can express, is the note of submergence into nothingness before an overpowering, absolute might of some kind . . . " (Otto 1958, 10).

This "submergence into nothingness" is central to the experience of feeling defiled before the daemonic sacred and the evoked affect of dread, implying as they do the threat of annihilation. The following from Otto, in which he describes the feelings of encountering the *tremendum*, could have been lifted from a psychological text on shame:

> It is the feeling of absolute "profaneness" . . . [which] comes with piercing acuteness, and is accompanied by the most uncompromising judgement of self-depreciation, a judgement passed, not upon his character, because of individual 'profane' actions of his, but upon his very existence as creature before that which is supreme above all creatures. . . . [The numen] is the positive *numinous* value or worth, and to it corresponds on the side of the creature a numinous *disvalue* or "unworth." (Otto 1958, 51)

We can see how the seeds of one's sense of defilement are contained here. The divine is absolutely real, absolutely supreme, and all-powerful. It follows that if all power is vested in the *tremendum*, all being is vested in it. The self, then, in this perspective is impotent, not essentially real, and whatever existence it has can be wiped out gratuitously, arbitrarily, because it is profane. We cannot know whether it is man's fear of quixotic annihilation or an attribute of the *tremendum* which gives rise to the idea of the Wrath of god, but the sense of a wrathful presence is a given in the numinous encounter and, indeed, in the history of religions. From Otto we hear that "This [wrath] is nothing but the *tremendum* itself, apprehended and expressed by the aid of a naïve analogy from the domain of natural experience, in this case from the ordinary passional life of men. . . . It is . . . 'like a hidden force of nature', like stored-up electricity, discharging itself upon anyone who comes too near. It is 'incalculable' and 'arbitrary'" (Otto 1958, 18).

It is of the nature of the dark side of the divine, Max Zeller tells us, to want to kill (Zeller 1990, 55)—a startling recognition reiterated by Ricoeur: "The Sacred is perceived, in the archaic stage of the religious consciousness, as that which does not permit a man to stand, that which makes him die" (Ricoeur 1967, 43). Annihilation is the punishment for being "less than," for creaturely defilement, and with defilement, says Ricoeur, "we enter into the reign of Terror" (ibid., 25), terror of being annihilated, terror at being in a state of defilement and thus becoming a locus of evil. In this ontic condition, dread permeates the archaic psyche: this is Otto's "numinous dread," or "daemonic dread," in the face of the *mysterium tremendum*, which "has its wild and demonic forms and can sink to an almost grisly horror and shuddering" (1958, 12). It aims "at a diminution of existence, a loss of the personal core of one's being" (Ricoeur 1967, 41).

As a result of feeling defiled at "the personal core of one's being," shame and dread exist as part of what one *is* and are not merely accompaniments to what one *does*. That is why I have sometimes modified "shame" with the adjective "ontic," to designate the radical, primal kind of shame on which we are focused here. It becomes part of our ontogenic history, a nuclear element which for the shamecarrier is as elemental as the color of one's eyes, as close as one's breath. And that is why shame can erupt in any of the sectors of reality.

This was vividly brought home to me recently when a friend asked, "Is there *any* activity which does not offer you the possibility of feeling shame?" After several moments, I could come up with only two such activities. This little exercise forced a recognition of how globally present the potential for shame is in my life—and, perhaps more helpfully, that that potential is *within me*, not in the outer world. But someone carrying this potential into the world is not unlike a person with an unprotected wound on the arm walking into a milling, insensitive throng; one has always the expectation that the wound will be crashed into, deepened, made to bleed, causing great pain.

We have already heard this place described by Hultberg: "Hell might be a state of eternal shame, shame that is overwhelming and all-consuming pain . . . implying utter physical destruction" (1988, 115). I could acknowledge the accuracy of his description because it matched so well what I had written in my journal:

> The sensation is of falling into the existential abyss, into the Great Void, a place of horror and unspeakable darkness which is both empty and not empty. This is not death; it is worse than death. It is the sense of being eternally tormented with no hope, ever, of release. Of being torn apart, annihilated, but at the same time being kept alive so that every smallest split-second of torment has to be experienced consciously.

I believe this is the same place Kleinian analyst Nini Herman courageously depicts in her autobiography, although she does not account for it as I do:

> This "spectre" . . . is a conglomeration, brewed of witch and demon, of volcanoes that erupt, mud and earthquakes that send down roaring landslides of sewage, of teeth in a distorted leer, of part-objects and phantoms daubed with our own sadism, which we spew up in response to experiencing an absence where there ought to be a mother. . . . Here is the stuff of our worst nightmares, of a "bad" LSD trip, the ogre who in pantomimes makes all the children scream, the Bad Fairy, or the murderer, strangler, rapist or intruder: a synthesis of such pure terror that words are almost bound to fail us. (Herman 1988, 152-3)

Sometimes this trauma is first experienced (or reiterated) after infancy. We may well ask whether this may not be the dark and dreadful place to which abused children are taken, often by a parent or other trusted adult who to one degree or another carries for the child the weight and authority of the *imago Dei*. For this child-victim it is as though the divine itself is thrusting her into defilement, revealing its dark, killing aspect without equivocation or dissembling. The sense of defilement in such a case is brutally amplified by confusion; one could say it constitutes a twin defilement: the child is at once subjected to literal defilement and forced into a defiling encounter with the daemonic; and because the trauma is caused by the parent-qua-god, the unspoken message is that the child is inherently unworthy *before god* or she would not be subjected to (chosen for) this experience. Moreover, there is nowhere for the child to go with her pain, no one to whom to turn for comfort and reassurance because the defilement has been created by the supreme authority in her life, or with the collusion of the supreme authority. At least as important as these is the archetypal linkage of premature and/or unwanted sexuality with defilement. As Ricoeur points out, sexuality which is not governed by rules relating to times, places, and behaviors is primordially defiling, and "virginity and spotlessness are as closely bound together as sexuality and contamination" (Ricoeur 1967, 29).

I believe these are among the key factors which produce the perseveration observed in incest victims and in the usually very long process of healing, or coming to terms with the trauma. It is also one way of understanding why incest victims feel deep ontic shame when logic would argue that as victims their dominant affect "should" be outrage at the perpetrator. I further believe that it is the repressed infantile memory of the daemonic sacred and the ensuing sense of defilement which accounts to some extent for the growing number of claims of childhood abuse, in particular those which include memories of "satanic ritual abuse," charges which often cannot be confirmed by the most diligent investigation. Whether or not there has been a physical invasion, *something* has happened in the child-adult relationship which reconstellated the primordial sense of defilement.

MATERNAL EMPATHY AND THE HOLDING ENVIRONMENT

"An absence where there ought to be a mother," Nini Herman's plaintive phrase, leads us to the penultimate element of the thesis, the issue of the holding environment created by the mother. Here the thesis of this book and most of previously received thought mesh almost perfectly, since most are in agreement that it is the mother's capacity for "reverie," her capacity to intuit, embrace, and "metabolize" the infant's affects and chaos, which determines much of the infant psyche's developmental path—whether it will lead to relative psychological health or to dis-ease.

Michael Fordham gives us a good description of "metabolizing":

> One of the important emotional interactions between a mother and her baby is that a mother is able to contain her infant's emotional life and, especially in the infant's states of distress, help the child to manage them by metaphorically digesting them herself and feeding them back to her infant in a way that the infant can

use. Thus, mental life is facilitated and emotional pain relieved for the baby. (Fordham 1985, 15)

If, however, the mother fails to metabolize, to provide a mirroring frame of reference, if her mirroring function is "unpredictable, unstable, anxiety-ridden or hostile; if her confidence in herself as a mother is shaky, then the . . . child has to do without a reliable frame of reference," and the result will be a "disturbance in the primitive 'self-feeling'" (Mahler 1968, 19). In harsher language, Kohut writes that the "bedrock of that nexus of factors that bring about certain psychological illnesses, particularly the narcissistic personality disorders" is "the fear of the cold, unempathic, often latently psychotic, at any rate psychologically distorted, self-object."

> True, behind the head of the Medusa lies the supposedly castrated genital of the woman. But behind the dreadful genital of the woman lies the cold, unresponding, nonmirroring face of a mother (or of a psychotic father who has usurped the mother's self-object functions) who is unable to provide life-sustaining acceptance for her child because she is depressed or latently schizophrenic or afflicted with some other distortion of her personality. (Kohut 1977, 189)

This text could be continued without wrenching meaning or thought by adding Nini Herman's comment,

> The infant mind will sense acutely, and be set awash by terror, when a mother's mind is reeling, or is wildly out of kilter, the more so since it will be highjacked to serve as a container for maternal distress. (Herman 1988, 153)

Such terror, "the stuff of our worst nightmares," produces a psychological distortion "which is incompatible with sufficient sanity" and which cannot be conveyed by the term "bad object."

> Any less afflicted parts of the personality are virtually crowded out to a thin periphery. The presence of this constellation, different in every case, rarely lets us rest by day or achieve peace of mind. Its continuous persecution can drive us to drink or crime, drug addiction,

suicide and every form of acting out. Here defences like denial, omnipotence, splitting and projection all have their early foundation. Here,
finally, fragmentation, with its mad Siren song, promising a reprieve
from this lurid visitation, lures us to that escape which will lead to the
madhouse. (Op. cit.)

It is very easy to read passages such as these as reasons to place all
responsibility and blame on the mother. It is easy to remain in the infantile position, even as adults, in which we demand perfection of a being we
know intellectually is at best another fallible human being like ourselves.
We forget that like every other creation we are part of nature, subject to
nature's patterns and seeming vagaries, and in forgetting that and laying
all our psychic ills at the mother's door, we do what would astonish us if
we saw it in other life forms: the acorn blaming the oak because its limbs
were misshaped by the wind. We forget that to blame is to forfeit freedom, since chronic blame sustains a negative bond, which in turn blocks
insight, clarity, and the growth which can take place only in the company
of responsibility for self.

It is difficult but imperative work to leave the infantile position with its
unconscious assumptions about maternal perfection—that is, to separate the
ego from the infantile—and to make the essential differentiation between the
personal mother and the archetypal energies to which all of us are subject. For
the gaze of the Gorgon may be *in* the personal mother but (unless the mother
is entirely psychotic) it is not the gaze *of* the mother. The importance of that
distinction cannot be overstated. (It is a distinction unavailable to the
metapsychologies which do not embrace the reality of the archetypes and must
therefore base all their theories and draw all their conclusions without reference
to the wider, transhuman realm. Perhaps this is the cause for the "anti-Mom"
attitude which has been so prevalent in the popular mind.) In making this
distinction we diverge from Wurmser's conviction that the infant's sense of
intrinsic unloveability derives from an unloving or insufficiently loving mother,
and that this accounts for shame. If the analyst holds this conviction, in fact,
the path of therapy can become diverted, since analysands who are certain that
they were indeed loved by their mothers are left standing at a paralyzing fork in
the road. To go in one direction—to agree with theory—they must override
their feelings. To go in the other—to disagree with theory and with the analyst—
may lead to a dead-end. Mother may indeed have loved us, insofar as her make-up

allowed her to love, *but love is not always the problem.* As Alice Miller says, the mother may love the child excessively "though not in the manner that he needs, and always on the condition that he presents his 'false self'" (A. Miller 1981, 14). The critical factor is whether the mother herself carries the stigmata of the Gorgon and has been unable, for whatever reason, to work it through, to make it conscious, so that in her eyes the infant sees only its own terror and dread.

It is also possible that the fear seen in the mother's eyes is her fear of not being a good-enough mother, a fear which could very well exist precisely because she loves her baby and is aware of her own woundedness. And it is possible that Margaret Mahler was correct in her assessment that there are certain infants for whom normal mothering is not enough.

> My own observations do not bear out the theories that implicate exclusively or even mainly the "schizophrenogenic" mother. . . . In constitutionally greatly predisposed oversensitive or vulnerable infants, normal mothering does not suffice to counteract the innate defect in the catalytic, buffering, and polarizing utilization of the human love object or mothering agency in the outside world for intrapsychic evolution and differentiation. (Mahler 1968, 47-8)

Neumann, too, held that constitutional factors in the infant must be taken into account: that "An intense early activation of the mother archetype can . . . be made possible by a *creative disposition characterized by an active archetypal image world*" (1990, 81; emphasis mine). Edinger also points out that "we must be particularly careful to do justice to both the personal historical factors and also the *a priori* archetypal factors" (1974, 39). Both reflect Jung's position, made clear in his introduction to Frances Wickes' work on the child psyche:

> Behind every individual father there stands the primordial image of the Father, and behind the fleeting personal mother the magical figures of the Magna Mater. These archetypes of the collective psyche, whose power is magnified in immortal works of art and in the fiery tenets of religion, are the dominants that rule the preconscious soul of the child and, when projected upon the human parents, lend them a fascination which often assumes monstrous proportions. (Jung 1966b, xxiii)

Taking all this into consideration, we still must not lose sight of the possibility that fetal or infant sensitivity is the *result* of what is going on with the mother. Alice Miller states, "It strikes me as quite likely that fear on the pregnant mother's part . . . could lead to great alertness (sensitivity) in the fetus" (Miller 1984, 244n).

To be able to understand and accept these possibilities later in life as an "accident" in our lives, as an aspect of our destiny bound up with this particular woman and as deriving from a suprapersonal source, obviates long and toxic years of blaming and places the issue not with another fragile human being but squarely where it belongs, with our responsibility and in the religious dimension. For at bottom, this is a religious issue. If understood well enough, it penetrates into many of the major issues of our lives: our capacity for compassion, our conviction of personal responsibility for who we are, our view of the source and nature of evil, our capacity for "catching up" developmentally and forming the crucial automorphic centers of self-respect, and our view of the relationship between the human and the divine.

The personal mother, or mothering figure, cannot, of course, be left entirely out of this equation, for the personality, the psychic configuration, of the mother has its effects on the inner archetypal world of the infant. This assertion is commonplace in Jungian psychology (e.g., Harding 1965), but Fordham's slightly different coloration makes his statement worth quoting:

> The relation between the ego, the self, and the unconscious as a whole, could be given primacy over a child's relation to his parents. It meant that, from very early in his life, the infant had boundaries other than those constructed during ego growth. They form the boundaries of an inner world built in the course of development, containing parent figures influenced by the real parents, but mainly imageing the unconscious archetypes. (Fordham 1962, 55)

From this we construe that the primary relationship of the infant is to the infant's inner world, not to the mother; the infant's inner world includes images of the archetypal mother and father; those images are influenced (changed) by the outer mother and father, respectively, but their centrality in the inner world continues to predominate over the importance of the outer parents. The relevance to the present thesis is, I think, clear: the infant's inner world of the archetypes includes some image of the daemonic sacred such as the Gorgon; the mother's inability to perceive and metabolize this dread and the presence in her own psyche of unattended chaos (depression, fear, etc.), influence the Gorgon image by strengthening it, by further delineating it; the *dynamis* of the image predominates over the outer mother's behaviors and feelings, no matter how mitigating they might otherwise have been.

A similar interpretation can be made of Kohut's observations concerning the disintegrative results of the "self-object's failures to be empathic with the whole self of the young child" (Kohut 1977, 247); among the products of this disintegration are shame and rage (ibid., 77). Disintegration experiences, if of sufficient magnitude and if prolonged, would return the infant to the site of the original catastrophe, in Ogden's words; of nameless dread, in Bion's; of chaos and the "psychotic" part of the psyche, in Klein's; to the place of encounter with the taboo sacred, the *tremendum*, and of defilement.

Identifying the Gorgon as the archetypal image polar to Aidos is not intended to suggest that the daemonic sacred is always and only feminine. Certainly the Greeks, as well as other cultures, sometimes imaged this aspect of the divine in masculine figures, for example the *daktyloi*—and, for that matter, some of the originally chthonian deities who made it to Olympos, including Zeus himself. However, the possibility still exists that the daemonic sacred is *au fond* feminine. There are good reasons to believe this may be so. Among those are that nature itself has from time immemorial been perceived as feminine; that the earliest religions were matrifocal or at least included female deities as an element at least as important as the male; the obvious archetypal centrality and potency of the mother, stemming in no small part from the human mother's physiological centrality; the fact that in the infant psyche the importance of the mother predates that of the father by several weeks, even to the point of experiencing the mother as *all* of reality, from which the father is excluded completely. However, what is most relevant here from the standpoint of psychology is pointed up by Nini Herman's comment:

> It is my personal conviction that this particular process [of the contents of one person's unconscious acting on another's unconscious

91

without passing through the conscious] is a specific function of maternal reverie and that even if it can and will affect the male, woman's susceptibilities to this phenomenon are considerably greater—a positive liability—and operate to a degree where it can deal life or death to so forceful an extent that it belongs to the uncanny. . . . (Herman 1989, 339)

From this it follows that the infant's experience of chaos, of the daemonic, will necessarily be assigned the feminine gender. Who can say this is not the reason why the Greeks came up with the Gorgon, the Erinyes, the Graiae, the Hindu tradition with Kali, and so forth. From Herman's comment, we can also deduce that the ontic shame which is our focus may be more likely to occur in girls than in boys. If that is so—and I am inclined to believe it is—it would provide a new and far-reaching way of understanding what have been perceived as women's passivity, vulnerability to victimization, and related issues such as creativity, self-assertion, depression, many of which have been understood in terms other than shame—for example, as problems associated with an undifferentiated or negative animus, with partriarchal repression, with negative parental introjects, to name just a few. None of these viewpoints lacks relevance or validity, but in certain cases they may neglect the radical cause.

In any case, the Gorgon happens to fall into place logically, initially because it is so intimately and powerfully linked with Athene, but also because of correlates between the effects of the Gorgon and the affects of shame—above all, those which make one feel frozen, paralyzed, turned to stone. Moreover, the Gorgon is the dominant surviving image of the very few images produced by Western culture which depict what Otto calls "a mysticism of horror." His central point in the following passage is a valuable reminder for us, even though he overlooks the Greek chthonic tradition altogether, and missteps a second time in equating the West exclusively with Christianity.

There has never been in the West a mysticism of horror, such as we find in certain kinds of Indian mysticism. . . . Yet, though the *tremendum* element in Christian mysticism is subdued, it is not entirely lacking. It remains a living factor in the *caligo* and the *altum silentium*, in the "abyss", the "night", the "deserts" of the divine nature, into which the soul must descend, in the "agony", "abandonment", "barrenness", *tae-*

dium, in which it must tarry, in the shuddering and shrinking from the loss and deprivation of selfhood and the "annihilation" of personal identity. (Otto 1958, 105)

But we need to return to the subject of the mother and the consequences of failure to create an empathic holding environment. Observations on this issue by clinicians working from their various perspectives are so familiar that it seems unnecessary to reiterate them. Suffice it to say that they can all be reasonably well summed up in the diagnostic label, "narcissistic disorder"—psychological dis-ease resulting from weakness or absence of the automorphic formations of self-esteem, self-respect, self-confidence. To those ways of understanding can be added a fresh and rewarding one from the discipline of philosophy, for which I am indebted primarily to the thought of Paul Ricoeur.

Ricoeur writes of a stage in the history of human development, with particular reference to ethics, an archaic stage "in which evil and misfortune have not been dissociated, in which the *ethical order of doing ill has not been distinguished from the cosmo-biological order of faring ill*: suffering, sickness, death, failure.... [P]unishment falls on man in the guise of misfortune and transforms all possible sufferings, all diseases, all death, all failure into a sign of defilement" (1967, 27). *only vaguely like more.*

If this is true of archaic man, and if the archaic psyche of the infant recapitulates that historical stage in the development of the species, then Ricoeur's assertion can reveal something about the process taking place in the young psyche facing an empathically deficient holding environment. The process put into words would be something of this sort: I am faring ill (my chaotic primitive emotions are not being metabolized and I continue to feel terror and dread), therefore I am *doing* ill, therefore it must be my nature to *be* ill, therefore I must be defiled. A similar "logic" will occur where the loving mother fears she will not be good enough; the "I am not a good mother" will at this time of unitary reality be indistinguishable to the infant from "I am not a good child." This occult syllogism is implied in received clinical thought, e.g., in Ogden's citation of Fairbairn, "The earliest experience of a 'lack of fit' between mother and infant leads the infant to feel that it is his or her way of loving that is hurtful" (1988, 648, n. 123), and in Winnicott's observations that maternal failures are felt by the infant to be not the mother's but the infant's own.

The infant, of course, does not yet have the equipment with which to cognize or to articulate the process in words, nor is the self-reflective capacity present as far as we know now. One of Thomas Ogden's comments suggests that the infant *undergoes* a psychological event without precisely "experiencing" it as the adult understands "experience." He writes:

> The "fear of breakdown" described by Winnicott (1974) represents a form of failure to generate experience in which the patient is terrified of experiencing for the first time a catastrophe that has already occurred. *The very early environmental failure that constituted the catastrophe could not be experienced at the time that it occurred, because there was not yet a self capable of experiencing it—that is, capable of elaborating the event psychologically, and of integrating it.* As a result, the patient forever fearfully awaits his own psychological breakdown. (Ogden 1989, 200; emphasis mine)

And as Kohut points out, in commenting on the "Kleinian fallacy," verbalizable fantasies are not present in earliest infancy; he asserts instead that this early state can be described in terms of tension increases and decreases (Kohut 1977, 101). However, we also have Winnicott's observations, cited earlier, that by the ninth month of gestation "there is already a human being in the womb, one that is capable of having experiences and of accumulating body memories and even of organizing defensive measures to deal with traumata" (1988, 143). Perhaps it is enough to say, in the face of these contradictions, that the process happens through the dance of instinct and shifts of affects—we could say it goes on through a kind of archetypal symbolic logic, in the same way that the infant can know the difference between the mother and a stranger, or between a female and a male (as infants do, prenatally [Restak 1986]), or between being safe and being abandoned.

This archaic process is not restricted to infants but continues, if not caught by a vigilant consciousness, throughout life. If we have an auto accident or a fall, for example, the archaic part of our psyche will ask if we are being punished for having done something or for *being* something wrong. In "New Age" perspective, the question is whether our *thinking* is wrong. Undoubtedly this ancient connection figures in the shame our culture attaches to illness, poverty, and the act of dying—all conditions we do not purposively bring about. Like the early Greek, we are "punished" for an unwitting, unconscious, and unintended "transgression." This question about *being* something wrong is the outcry identified by Wurmser in his discussion of unloveability as the sense of "a fundamental a priori cursedness":

> "Why have I been born so that I do things and am so that the gods and mankind have to extrude me as unacceptable and unlovable and treat me as a monstrous aberration? . . . " This seems to be the outcry of an Oedipus, of a Philoctetes, of a Hamlet. . . . We saw it as the abyss of primal shame. (Wurmser 1995, 292)

We have to assume that this process takes place at the deepest layer of the psyche, since that layer is coextensive with the archetypal, psychoid realm, is present in the archaic mind, and is instinct with the most fundamental ontological issues, of existence, of creation, of the origins of life, of the relationship of the human to the divine. The process has been traced by clinicians but at the next layer up, so to speak, where the issues deal with the "primary relationship" of mother and child, and the conclusion reached is basically that the nascent self is crippled because of the mother's empathic failures. But the true primary relationship is between the created and the Creator, and the most far-reaching effect of empathic failures is probably the effect on the individual's relationship to the Self and to the divine.

Here in the infant is a psyche without ego, without language, without sophisticated defenses, who has looked upon, or is looking upon the transcendent, for whom mother is "thou, world and Self in one" (Neumann 1990, 86), and is therefore the *only* antidote for the primitive terror constellated by the inner numinous vision. The absence or inadequacy of that antidote is tantamount to confirmation that the sacred *is* terrifying, that there is no recourse, absolution, security, or hope anywhere in the cosmos, and that the infant truly is a defiled being. Spiritually, then, the infant is in the existential condition of primitive man, for whom the numinous, the sacred, is always experienced in its wild, demonic form, uncanny, eerie, weird, before which one can only shudder with terror, and before which one feels one's creaturehood in the most negative possible way, as defilement. If we accept that the Self bears the imprint of the *imago Dei*, and if the divine image is from life's inception one which inspires unmitigated terror, it follows that the ego-

Self relationship, whether understood psychologically or theologically, is radically impaired, not to say obviated altogether. The very Self becomes a source of terror, and the formation of the ego will be, to paraphrase Hart Crane, wrenched into defensive anatomies. This is a tragic loss of the true self for the individual, but it is moving testimonial to the strength of the human spirit that *any* ego, even a heavily adaptive one, can be formed in the face of such odds.

As life goes on, two forces work on the imprint of this process, pulling in opposite directions but both obliterating its conscious memory. One force works to mitigate or repress the imprint; it comprises scores of experiences both intrapsychic (such as ego formation and setting up of defense mechanisms) and extrapsychic (absorption in developmental tasks, relationship experiences, etc.). If we grow up in the Judaeo-Christian tradition, the daemonic sacred is wholly obscured by the emphasis on the total benevolence of god. All these serve to repress the original experience, but it returns, usually subtly, in situations which activate the archaic psyche. How many of us confronted with a misfortune have not felt, even fleetingly, the suspicion that we are being punished for a transgression (or for too much success), that god does not love us, that we must be unworthy of good fortune or love—that we are defiled.

The other force, which also works to bury the source of the wound but simultaneously reinforces and reiterates its effects, is made up of every shame experience, of which there is an abundance even in the most ordinary of lives—in all the sectors of reality mentioned in the first chapter, touching upon body, intellect, relationships, appearance, skills, our very selves.

Ironically, these two forces, although working in seemingly opposite directions, work to close a circle which binds us captive, for they perpetuate the conflict between the all-powerful god and the defiled creature: in psychological terms, they perpetuate the adaptive ego and the break in the ego-self axis. It is my experience and my conviction that the reason the affect of ontic shame runs so deeply, floods the self, and becomes global so quickly, the reason there is so often a wide discrepancy between the triggering event and the reaction, the reason the affect plunges us into a hellish abyss, is that what we call a "shaming experience" reaches down into and feeds the fires of the primordial wound of creaturely defilement. To restate that imagetically, the shaming experience feeds the Gorgon which sits at our center, killing us with the look of its glaring, death-dealing eyes.

It may even be this presence and its life-denying function which sometimes lies at the bottom of many of the concepts developed by the metapsychologies: e.g., Klein's "paranoid position," with its conviction that the environment is essentially hostile; Bion's "nameless dread" and "persecutory anxiety"; Wurmser's "defect of intrinsic unlovability"; Kohut's "disintegration anxiety"; Neumann's "negative Self image." It may, indeed, be at the root of psychosis, for in these chaotic winds the ego experiences the dire threat of fragmentation and dissolution, accompanied by a terror that the defenses will not hold. No doubt this worst of all existential torments accounts, at least in part, for the fact that it is a rarely heard primal memory. As Herman says, "To take an unflinching look into the heart of the crater of this catastrophe [she labels it "the devastation of the psychotic parts of the personality," or areas of chaos] takes heroic courage. . . . For that reason it will either remain hidden or only surface in disguise and so finely fragmented that it may well be missed [by the analyst]" (Herman 1988, 152).

Despite the general agreement among clinicians that the unresponsive post-natal environment "pushes" the infant psyche back into the inner chaos, I find it difficult to accept the "chaos" as simply an absence of order in the infantile psyche. There must be a presence and a source for the presence, a way of accounting for it, specially in view of Winnicott's and Kohut's suggestions of rudimentary organization. Jungian psychology accounts for it through the theory of archetypes; Neumann, most notably, asserts that the failure of the mother to constellate the archetype of the Great Mother, "her defection," as he puts it, "transforms the world into chaos and nothingness . . . leaving the child utterly lonely and forlorn, or becomes an enemy and persecutor, while the child's own Self is transformed into a representative of the Terrible Mother" (1990, 86-7). This understanding, I have no doubt, is valid as far as it goes. But it falls short of explaining why the entire experience is suffused with such powerful numinosity; why, if it surfaces to consciousness later in life, it is consistently depicted in imagery and diction revolving around the divine; why the destructive energies described are so powerful as to transcend the human. Why does the infant psyche experience the threat of annihilation rather than simple distress or discomfort? Why does it experience chaos and not just confusion? Why does fear become terror, anger become rage, and why does insecurity reach into persecution? In short, why does this experience push beyond the level of plain human negativity all the way to the rim of the existential abyss?

Reason alone argues agreement with Otto's assertion that the feeling of the numinous "is a primal element of our psychical nature that needs to be grasped purely in its uniqueness and cannot itself be explained from anything else. Like all other primal psychical elements, it *emerges* in due course in the developing life of human mind and spirit and is thenceforward simply present" (1958, 124). Similarly, von Franz asserts that "the human psyche is structured to produce" archetypal images and fantasies which have "the same feature of being unnatural, super-human, gruesome and overwhelming" (1983, 125). Had Otto been a Jungian psychologist, he would have said that among the archetypes is an archetype of the divine. Without such an "imprint" in the psyche, we have to ask, how would we ever have evolved the idea of god, since there is nothing in ordinary sensory experience to suggest god's existence. This, in fact, supports the validity of the belief that we are born with a memory, with Neumann's "mythological apperception," with innate, *a priori* ideas which permit the early recognition that the numinous has been encountered. It's as though the psyche were an artifact of handblown glass; after the glass has cooled and the form sufficiently congealed, the blower's breath and the tube are withdrawn, but the pontil mark remains, an imprint of our origins and of our first participation in what is the primary relationship with the source of life. Unless we give credence to this idea, how do we explain the fact that we so often recognize the meaning of certain symbols without having been instructed in their meaning. We have to be taught the meaning of signs—much of formal education consists of memorizing connections between signs and their referents—but the rich, resonant content of symbols often seems to be something we know innately.

Even Freud seems to have hovered around the idea of an infantile encounter with the dark aspect of the sacred. Writes Herman,

> What is it . . . that is concealed when we start to feel uncanny? Freud concludes that the feeling fundamentally "proceeds from *forms of thought that have been surmounted,*" and that the uncanny is due to those elements which play a part "in the production of infantile

anxiety from which the majority of human beings have never become quite free." (1989, 21; emphasis mine)

Winnicott acknowledges that "It is as though some babies are born paranoid, by which I mean in a state of expecting persecution" (1988, 149).

The concept of infantile anxiety leads us to the final element of the thesis: chronic, pervasive dread.

DREAD

Dread, Ricoeur asserts, is the internalization of defilement (1968, 101); it "deserves to be interrogated as our oldest memory" (ibid., 30). It is the affect aroused by awareness of our impurity and weakness in the face of the purity and terrible power of the sacred and is "an instrument by which the defiled self becomes conscious of itself." Dread, he says, "faces a threat which . . . aims at a diminution of existence, a loss of the personal core of one's being" (ibid., 41).

I am suggesting that the disintegrative aspect of shame, which feels as though it would annihilate our existence, more properly bears the name "dread." The use of these two labels to denote degrees of "shame" would, it seems to me, add considerable clarity. "Shame" might be reserved for the relatively shallow affects of embarrassment which nearly everyone feels now and then—at, for example, mispronouncing a word, forgetting someone's name, discovering a spot on one's lapel, performing badly on a test. But when the affect is so profound that it penetrates into that dark place of paralysis and terror, it deserves to be called dread.

In this condition, we as adults suffer the affects of the infantile, archaic psyche, the anxiety Winnicott traces to our earliest months:

> Maternal failures produce phases of reaction to impingement [disturbances of the infant's sense of existential continuity] and these reactions interrupt the 'going on being' of the infant. An excess of this reacting produces not frustration but a *threat of annihilation*. This in my view is a very real primitive anxiety, long antedating any anxiety that includes the word death in its description. . . . The mother's failure to adapt in the earliest phase does not produce anything but an annihilation of the infant's self. . . . Her failures are not felt [by the infant] as maternal failures, but they act as threats to personal self-existence. (Winnicott 1988, 303-4)

99

Too many of us live in this condition every day of our lives; dread has become chronic and pervasive. Encounters with strangers are fraught with hazard we often allow to be only semiconscious. Relationships with intimates offer the possibilities of being wounded, rejected, found inadequate. Association with authority figures such as employers puts us in the powerless, "down" position because our lives, our livelihoods, are held in the hands of someone who may find us incompetent or unworthy, or simply dispensable, and who has the power to destroy our career or even our life as we have known it. We live provisional lives, with a perpetual "what if," in dread that our essential inadequacy and worthlessness will be discovered and that we will be annihilated because of it.

My most recent experience of this searing affect happened when I discovered that I had given an incorrect budget figure to my employer. The figure had no great significance, my employer is a humane and gentle man, and I was alone in the office when I made the discovery, but at that moment I was instantaneously plunged into the heat of the "existential blush," swamped by the affect. My thoughts, such as they were, became chaotic and disappeared altogether in the raw heat of terror; it was as though a supremely powerful and malignant presence were in the room with me, its gaze peeling me down to nakedness so that my "real" stupidity and rottenness would have no cover. What would have been a mild embarrassment for someone else—or merely a signal to make a correction—was for this shamecarrier a source of inner degradation. It is a shamecarrier's typical experience, illustrative of the enormous disparity between the triggering event and the radical, global, primordial affect. For the shamecarrier, even a spot on the lapel can be demonic.

It can be readily seen why perfectionism, to mention just one defense, becomes one of our favorites. If imperfection is the threat, the armor against it is to be perfect. Society happens to like this defense. It makes for good children, good employees, good neighbors, good students. And, of course, it plays wonderfully well into the Judaeo-Christian ethic, with its emphasis on "moral" behavior. Unfortunately, it is one of the worst defenses the shamecarrier could construct, because it sets up standards which usually escalate over the years and which, being impossible to meet, serve only to compound the problem, since standards of perfection simply create more definitions of imperfection and thus more occasions for failure. Ricoeur reminds us that "the great discovery of [the biblical] Paul is that the law itself is a source of sin. . . . [T]he law is that which exhibits sin, that which makes sin manifest" (1967, 140).

A central implication of all this is that if the power to annihilate has been located in the partner, the employer, the friend, even in the passing stranger, then somehow, somewhere along the line, the external other has been put *in loco Dei*. Doing this, we imitate the patriarchal Athene, the Father's Daughter; our unconscious definition of *aidos* is Homer's definition, tied to the collective, so that we derive a sense of worth and honor from how we are perceived rather than from what we are. This location would seem to be a deeply unconscious continuation of the infant's original experience of the maternal environment, in which, as we have seen, for the infant the mother holds the power of life and death and carries the *imago Dei*. When we extend the infantile position in this way into later life, we tend unconsciously to seek the Good Mother and/or god in our life partners, our employers, even in our social and cultural environment. Failures in those persons and structures are then unconsciously experienced as failures of the divine—god turning away from us because we are unworthy, a reiteration of our primordial defilement and the dread of being annihilated. It is a reiteration that will continue as long as the primal experience of the daemonic sacred remains unconscious and/or our relationship to the sacred remains inchoate.

This configuration constellates the inner Gorgon, its death-dealing gaze fixed not on the outer world but on our inmost selves. At bottom it is not the outer threat we dread so much as the involuntary return to our inner infantile terror, the dread which Otto calls daemonic, and which prowls the halls of the infantile psyche. This dread of stirring the Gorgon, this terror of reinstituting the primordial defilement, is analogous if not identical to what Ogden describes in the passage cited above: we are "terrified of experiencing for the first time *a catastrophe that has already occurred.*"

This is in part my reason for saying earlier that shame can be read as a symbol in that it points the way to something else: it is the affect created by the dread of experiencing the catastrophe which has already occurred but the memory of which has remained unconscious, buried in the deep layers of the archaic psyche and the somatic self. The dread we feel is the primordial dread of an annihilation which has already been threatened and which is still going on if it is not stopped in its tracks by working to make it conscious: the annihilation of the original self. For to lose the original self is to be in a state of non-being—the kind of non-being on which Jung comments in this passage on the Gorgon aspect of Persephone:

> We could say that through the figure of Persephone, the stately Queen of Hades, we glimpse the Gorgon. What we conceive philosophically as the element of *non-being* in Persephone's nature appears, mythologically, as the hideous Gorgon's head, which the goddess sends forth from the Underworld and which she herself bore in her archaic form. It is not, of course, *pure* non-being, rather the sort of non-being from which the living shrink as from something *with a negative sign*: a monstrosity that has usurped the place of the unimaginably beautiful, the nocturnal aspect of what by day is the most desirable of all things. (Jung 1969, 127-8)

Ricoeur states boldly that the experience of non-being *is the experience of evil* (1986, xxvii). From Jung's comments we can rightly, I think, assume that he would have agreed. If we look at these remarks in terms of the original self and the adapted, shamecarrying, "false" self, we must conclude that the original self, whose place has been usurped by the shamecarrying self, is "unimaginably beautiful." For it *not to be*—that is, for it not to be allowed expression in life—is an experience of evil, soul murder. To the degree that we are identified with the adapted, shamecarrying self, we perpetuate the original catastrophe, the soul murder, and to that degree we are in collusion with evil; "evil entails being swept away by one-sidedness, by only *one single* pattern of behavior" (von Franz 1983, 147). We are, in effect, in collusion with the Gorgon.

From this perspective, the Gorgon may be seen as a form of what von Franz terms natural evil, "which does not pose any ethical problem but the purely practical one of how to either overcome it or successfully escape it" (ibid., 122). That problem is the focus of the final chapter, where we return to our mythic triad to see where we are led, whether towards escape or conquest.

Chapter Four

Turning the Gorgon

Une difficulté est une lumière./Une difficulté insurmontable est un soleil. ✿
— Paul Valéry

In the end that Face which is the delight or terror of the universe must be turned upon each of us either with one expression or with the other, either conferring glory inexpressible or inflicting shame that can never be cured or disguised.
— C. S. Lewis, in *They asked for a paper*

We have come this far in our meditation: we have looked at various clinical and theoretical perspectives on shame; we have surveyed early Greek thought about *aidos* in its changing cultural context; we have retrieved something of the nature of Athene hidden beneath the patriarchal overlays; and we have explored an etiology of shame which redefines its affect as dread, giving it the image of the Gorgon whose apotropaic powers, instead of being protectively turned outward, are destructively turned inward upon the self. Here and there along that sometimes circuitous road have been signposts suggesting, if not cure, ways of doing our lives differently—of forming new perspectives, of trading some values for others, of working to generate or enhance those early automorphic formations of self-esteem and self-love that are so crucial to wholeness, life, love of others. Just as the journey behind led us through three seemingly discrete realms of thought—mythology, psychology, and religion—so shall the one ahead, intertwining the three realms, as they are in psychic reality. What I hope to do in the pages ahead is to share with the reader the possibilities which have presented themselves to me, possibilities of responding in healthier, more life-affirming ways to one's condition as a shamecarrier. If this implies "healing," it does so in the sense defined by Carotenuto:

> [as] substantially a matter of making available to the ego an internal reserve of energy sufficient to increase automorphic feelings and cure depression related to the primary sense of guilt. (Carotenuto 1992, 105)

Automorphic feelings, as we know by now, are those "not originating in the relationship with another person, e.g., self-respect, self-affirmation, self-confidence, senses of responsibility and security" (ibid., 104).

TURNING THE GORGON: A MYTHIC APPROACH

We begin by returning to the image with which we left the last chapter, the Gorgon, and to the goddess with whom the Gorgon is most associated, Athene. Here we have on the one hand the perfect emblem of terror and dread and on the other a deity whose person embodies markedly positive characteristics: protective concerns for humanity combined with a sharp sense of boundaries; creativity and imagination combined with a pragmatic realism; respect for the inner world combined with a capacity for vigorous extraverted action; developed feeling with no trace of sentimentality; innate, instinctive wisdom paired with discursive intellection; maternality paired with autonomy; and, most important of all, the strength of androgynous wholeness. No less than the Judaeo-Christian divine, she is an expression of the *coincidentia oppositorum*, a being in whom the opposites co-exist. And it can be argued that of all the Greek deities she most provided the experience of the numinous, since she was closest and appeared most frequently to humankind.

For her wholeness more than any other reason, Athene deserves to be contemplated as emblematic of the Self; from her original, unconditioned, pre-patriarchal person it is possible to learn something about the nature of one's original, true self. She can be for us what she was for Odysseus, "a most beautiful expression of the feminine power of inspiration and guidance through the trials of the world" (Jaeger 1945, 1:24). As a symbol of the Self, she is, in Esther Harding's words, also a symbol of wholeness, "able to confront its opposite, the chaos, without disintegration" (Harding 1965, 233).

In looking at the relationship between this Athene-Self and the Gorgon, we will first remember that Athene had been nursed and tended not by an unempathic or latently psychotic mother (or by an irascible, quixotic, inflated Father Zeus), but by the goddess Aidos, the embodiment of reverence, aweful respect. Certainly an infant in such a "holding environment" is mothered by someone who is able to digest chaos, who can provide the empathic surround in which the automorphic centers can develop without impediment. This is the critical factor in the character of Athene's successful dealings with the Gorgon; it is the differential factor between the shamecarrier so chronically devastated by the inward-gazing Gorgon and the Athene-Self who deploys the Gorgon in its apotropaic and prophylactic functions.

What did this Athene do with the Gorgon that we might consider as a useful model in our own lives? To put the question another way, how would the original, unconditioned self, supported by relationship to the wholeness of the Self, address ontic shame and dread and the terrors of annihilation?

For our purposes, the commonly known version of the Athene-Medousa myth can be reduced to four basic mythemes: (1) Athene sent Perseus to slay the Gorgon; (2) she aided him by lending her shield and by guiding his hand for the fatal blow; (3) she deployed the Gorgon's power in two very disparate ways, to destroy and to sustain life; (4) she honored the daimon by wearing its skin as her *aegis*. We shall explore these in sequence for their implications.

The dispatching of Perseus can be understood as Athene's ability to differentiate and to deploy the heroic and "masculine" aspects of her androgynous self for the purpose of depotentiating an aspect of the daimonic feminine which had become berserk, a monster. We have seen that as the Olympian view grew in ascendancy the old chthonian, matriarchal order was not simply devalued but was increasingly linked with all that was anathema to the rationalistic new patriarchal order: nature, mystery, nonrationality, "chaos." The daimon Gorgon, repressed and derogated, finds herself in the situation described by von Franz: "The destructive emotionality which is so easily connected with evil in a masculine type of civilization causes the feminine principle to be destructive" (1983, 271). The balance-loving Athene, by depotentiating the berserker extreme of the Gorgon, achieves two fundamental things: she rescues the Gorgon's energy from the one-sidedness into which it had fallen, a one-sidedness in which it was gratuitously destructive of whatever came into view, without discriminating what was appropriate and what was not; and she returns the Gorgon to its original apotropaic function, which is to say to its dual role as protector and destroyer, thereby restoring order in that this aspect of the chthonian has been returned to a functional place in the scheme of things. Through Perseus, she has accomplished what von Franz indicates in a continuation of the passage cited above:

> If that principle—the anima or feminine principle—is brought up from Hell into consciousness, it overcomes the specific form of evil represented here [in the fairy tale under discussion] as the devil. The new principle of consciousness then dwells . . . in a center of totality beyond the split between good and evil. (Op. cit.)

In the second mytheme, Athene's assistance to Perseus, what seems the most striking element is Athene's loaning of her shield, which is to be used not in the conventional way, to ward off, but *as a mirror*. That Athene's shield would reflect the Gorgon may be understood symbolically as a tacit acknowledgement of a covert kinship between the goddess and the *daimon*. We have already pointed out that both are chthonian in origin, having as they do their roots in a feminine-dominated religion; that insofar as both are sprung from the Great Mother both are androgynous (although it may be more accurate to say that the Gorgon was bisexual); that in the original Greek the same word is used to describe both sets of eyes; that in certain myths both are said to have come from Libya; that in at least one myth both were said to have been fathered by Poseidon, making them half-sisters; that both were connected with horses—as, of course, was Poseidon. All of which is to say that there is a certain amount of evidence supporting the idea of their kinship. Again symbolically, Athene's actions can be read as a reclaiming of and raising to consciousness a part of her original nature, her chthonic, pre-patriarchal, nonrational, profoundly natural and familial relation to the feminine principle. Paradoxically, this can be claimed only by "killing" it *in the form to which it had been distorted*, in keeping with the truth that in every achievement of consciousness, something must die.

The third mytheme, the dual deployment of the Gorgon's power, derives from the motif of the two vials of the Gorgon's blood, one of which kills, the other of which heals. While this may appear merely to underscore the ambivalent nature of the daimon, it does add a positive where before there was only a negative (the berserker aspect) and is a recognition of wholeness. By raising the Gorgon to consciousness and restoring her to her proper place in the natural order, Athene makes apparent and available the transformative, curative aspect of what was one-sidedly monstrous as long as it remained in "Hell" (i.e., repressed and devalued). Athene not only restored the Gorgon to her proper place but restored her to her original status in the old religion, in which she was "a potent goddess, not as in later days a monster" (Harrison 1991, 194) whose eye was not itself the Evil Eye but "the prophylactic Eye, the eye set to stare back the Evil Eye" (ibid., 196).

Incidentally, by Plato's time, if not earlier, this double aspect of the daimonic had made its way into philosophical thought. Plato says that a man may have a "bad" daimon and/or a "good" one. The good one crept into English in our word "eudemonia," meaning happiness or well-being.

What are in the third mytheme honorific implications become quite overt in the fourth and final mytheme, in which Athene adopts as part of her garb the Gorgon's head (variously, the entire skin). With this act, the goddess proclaims to the world her inherent kinship with the chthonian daimon and the functional presence of that kind of power as companion to the discursive power of the rational intellect. In other words, she proclaims her wholeness.

We must not overlook the fact that Athene does not wear the *gorgoneion* as a mask. Athene is never to my knowledge depicted with her head or face covered by mask or helmet; she uses the *gorgoneion* protectively but not defensively.

From Athene's actions we can learn a great deal about "turning the Gorgon" in our lives. We can ask ourselves, first, whether we are aware of and willing to embrace the fact of our essential psychological androgyny, the so-called contrasexual elements of our psyches. (I say "so-called" be-cause this terminology is threatening to some people and to my mind unnecessarily compartmentalizes attributes which then become either over-valued or undervalued as inherently "feminine" or "masculine." I know this is a time-honored and orthodox Jungian concept, and that it continues

107

to serve an important purpose, but I wish we could replace it with the much more embracing and less gender-fixated Chinese concept of yin and yang: forces of nature, one actively receptive, the other actively assertive, both resident in all of creation.) If we are, we may next ask whether we have enough clarity (consciousness) to differentiate those elements and to deploy them *without affect* in the service of wholeness. If we do, then our inner Perseus can be sent not to sickle off the inner Gorgon's head but to depotentiate its berserker aspect, to some degree at least, by raising it to consciousness.

Just reading this book and giving consideration to its premises may be one way of deploying the hero energy—of locating the heroic aspect of the original self, which is able to look dread in the eyes in an effort to bring it out of the dark and to understand it. Just to arrive at the knowledge that the Gorgon is *there* is an act of heroism. Committing to analytical work is another approach to the Gorgon, one which always requires quiet courage if it is undertaken with serious commitment. Athene's mirror-shield is an apt image of the analytical process, which can enable one to confront and experience the dragon not in a shattering face-to-face solitary exposure but through reflection in the empathic holding environment of the analytical relationship. This is almost without exception the wisest course for any of us who are shamecarriers. Facing the Gorgon, as we know, is a hazardous undertaking and best ventured in the company of one who has already been to "the edge of the Deep Canyon" and come back unharmed—or at least stronger and wiser. Moreover, to get there one must travel through the country of the personal shadow, always a ticklish business but specially so for the shamecarrier: the personal shadow holds repressed negative aspects of the personality (or aspects perceived as negative), psychic contents which can add to the already huge burden of shame, defilement, and dread. It is good to have with us a guide who is able to help us assimilate these contents—and who can point out the positives. Since most of our tribe have over the years developed an adaptive ego and defenses of compliance, perfectionism, and so forth, the personal shadow is likely to have less lead in it than gold—positive traits of the buried original self—but we are apt to pass over those positive traits without seeing them, being blinded by our need for defense; or we may see the gold but be too frightened to claim it, since to lay claim some of our most cherished defenses would have to be abandoned. To claim it would also mean the integration of parts of the original self which have already been condemned as defiled, undesirable. In short, it would mean individuating, claiming and being who we uniquely are whether or not that always meets with social acceptance or conforms to the collective.

Athene's actions also suggest the importance of admitting one's kinship to the Gorgon—that is, that we ask what our relationship is to shame and dread. Do we, for example, collaborate with the Gorgon by agreeing with her messages of unworth and defilement, falling unconsciously into the victim position and refusing to claim the gold of the original self? Do we deny any relationship to her by trying to ignore, distract, override her? Or by projecting her? Do we feed her berserker aspect by acting out unconscious rage and aggression, inevitable products of the infantile wound—and by acting out, add yet another layer of shame when we finally reflect on that behavior? (How much of the Gorgon's monstrosity and potency for annihilation is our own primitive rage?) Or do we, like Athene, claim her and the wound from which she was birthed, thereby making possible her transformation? If this is our capacity and our choice, the next question is: how can we, like Athene, turn the Gorgon back to her apotropaic and prophylactic functions, so that she will protect us rather than destroy us? How can we restore her to her proper place in the natural order, honor her positive aspect, and obtain the vial which contains the curative blood?

To translate those questions into less metaphorical language, how can dread and shame be seen in a positive light? Some of the deeper responses to this question are examined below, when we return to the areas of psychology and religion, but there are responses to be made out of the mythic material as well.

We said that Athene, by taking up the Gorgon as part of her own image, proclaimed to a patriarchal culture her origins in, her kinship with, the old chthonian order. That would be the equivalent, for us, of individuating out of the collective. Fundamentally, that means that we are willing to: devote time and energy to discovering our original self; become aware of the nature of our defense mechanisms and drop or modify them if they serve only the demands of the collective and our needs for protection and not the real life of the original self; and acknowledge and embrace our

109

chthonic nature. Each of these activities is complex and cannot, to say the least, be accomplished overnight. Each can be amplified almost infinitum, but it is the last of them on which I want to add a few comments.

By our chthonic nature, I mean, of course, the aspects of our status as a human being which are closest to the instinctive, the animal, the material, the childlike, the earth. These are at the greatest remove from the discursive, abstract, and intellectual, the arena which often provides defensive refuge for the shamecarrier. In distancing ourselves from the chthonic, we sacrifice our connection with the roots of spontaneity, creativity, freedom of authentic expression, and relatedness. To return to and reclaim the chthonic in us is to return to our native soil. This movement may require what I have for some time considered as one antidote for shame: humility. Not the weak, milkish "humility" of victimhood or the false humility of self-effacement, but the humility implied by the word's root: *humus*, earth. This is the humility which realistically recognizes the human being's ontological location, which is, as Kant put it, midway between god and nothingness. The person of humility knows her condition of creaturehood as precisely midway: not god, but infused with the divine; not nothing, Abraham's "dust and ashes," who is then driven to compensate by erecting defenses, mechanisms which perpetuate the destructive aspects of the Gorgon. In this middle position, dread can be seen as a signal of our need to examine and accept what it means to be fully and truly human. In this sense, dread performs a curative function and through that transformation becomes the prophylactic Gorgon, preventing us from being dust and ashes at one extreme, keeping us at the other from falling into compensatory inflation, identification with the divine. It keeps us from falling into evil, which as we have seen originally meant going beyond the proper limits.

Wearing the *gorgoneion*, then, signifies having reclaimed our native soil and being sufficiently grounded in it to be able to look out upon the world with the helmet open—perhaps always there and always available, but open. It signifies that we are protected by the certitude of who we deeply are and of our value—that we are no longer defended by pretending to be who we are not. It signifies that we have chosen life, however hard-won and hazardous the choice may have been—and may still be, every day. That we have transformed the death-dealing energy of the berserker Gorgon into a life-giving *dynamis*; that we have found our "good daimon" in ourselves. What was a defensive mask, made necessary by dread of annihilation, has become a protective *aegis*, the skin of depotentiated dread.

The distinction between *protection* and *defense* is a fairly subtle one in practice. Self-protection is an expression of the Eros function since, although it is protective, it still lies within the sphere of relationship. It implies a number of things, among them that our awareness *of being in relation to* has continued within a context of legitimate discrimination, in which we have asked "Do I know this person well enough to be completely open with him?"; and that we value and know ourselves well enough to protect what may be specially vulnerable, or tender, or treasured. Athene did not sit *unarmed* at the innermost center of the house she guarded. Von Franz makes essentially the same point in her discussion of learning to trust one's naïve reactions: "One just needs the courage, being somewhat shrewd at the same time, so that one does not expose oneself to those people who do not understand. One should be clever and not just childish" (1981, 100).

In contrast, defense operates outside the Eros function. It breaks and makes impossible any real relatedness—to others, since it isolates us behind a barricade, making our authentic self inaccessible; and to our own self, since psychic energy is being used to sustain the defensive position rather than to nourish the ego-self connection.

It would be inappropriate to leave this discussion of Athene without looking again at her attributes and asking whether or not they contain some clues to what shamecarriers may expect to find in that buried treasure of the original self, where our potential for wholeness lies. Certainly one of those attributes will be Athene's capacity for direct action based on her reflective but sure-footed perceptions. Shame carriers have rarely experienced this capacity. Efforts to avoid precipitating shame, the need to comply, and the ever-present dread of annihilation force shamecarriers to process almost every thought, every feeling, every action, every situation, two, three, four times in their minds before feeling more or less ready to move into speech, action, life. Shamecarriers are not typically spontaneous, and it is common to regret the rare times when we have been (why did I say that? I should have said, I should not have said, I should have worn a different suit, they must think I am dull/stupid/insensitive, I wish I hadn't, ad infinitum). I have described this as the "stuttering of the soul," an impediment which keeps us from being fully engaged in our own lives,

111

keeps us living always *provisionally*, in that state T. S. Eliot knew was "living and partly living." The call to change this is articulated by Carotenuto:

> One must be audacious enough to consciously live one's shadow side, otherwise one really and truly sins against oneself—a sin that can never be forgiven. The basic question we must ask ourselves in drawing up the balance sheet of our lives is this: "Did I live as I really was?" If I cannot answer yes, I have not truly lived. (Carotenuto 1989, 100)

For the shamecarrier, consciously to live one's shadow is often to live traits which are positive, not only in the conventional sense of being socially and culturally desirable, but in the psychological sense of manifesting life and expressing self in the world. There are times, of course, when these do not coincide, when even a positive trait (such as loyalty to one's tastes and values) is not socially acceptable. In such instances, we are ideally able to overcome dread sufficiently to decide which is more important, acceptance of the ego personality or the life of the self, and then to anticipate what the cost of that decision will be and whether we can pay it. This kind of soul activity is part of the process by which we "individuate"— emerge as a unique individual out of but still within a collective context. Carotenuto (1992) very helpfully describes individuation as a series of processes involving (1) differentiation, which allows us to disidentify with the contents of the collective mind and to detach from the contents which are not part of our individuality, and (2) integration of those contents that should not be rejected but "ascribed in an original way to our own personalities" (61).

Another of Athene's attributes is her ability to "shift shapes"—to sustain her essential integrity of identity while expressing whatever aspect of self is appropriate to the situation or to her goals. Again, this is a capacity often unavailable to the shamecarrier and one which we may therefore assume is locked away in the shadow. Most of us have identified a few personality aspects which work best for us as defenses, or as compensation, or as safe masks in the world. The other aspects are often hidden, sometimes from ourselves as well as from others. The result is that we live much more narrowly than we need to—and may be perceived more narrowly by others who cannot experience the faceted richness which lies beneath the relatively monochromatic surface. Our dread keeps us in this constricted state, which is not unlike the one-sidedness to which von Franz refers and the situation described by David L. Miller:

> As long as we persist in asserting one power over others [e.g., we may emphasize our intellectual powers to the neglect of our feeling life, or vice versa], we will lose the richness and depth of having multiple resources, but we will also thereby eventually lose even the one power. . . . The clue from Athena is to make a place for them all, when they wish to appear as resources of meaning. (D. Miller 1981, 53)

Creativity is a dominant hallmark of Athene's person and an energy which must logically lie within the original self of the shamecarrier since it is inevitably repressed and strangulated by dread in the constrained, adaptive self. What Perera says of the "scapegoat-identified" person in the following passage can equally well be said of us when the death-dealing Gorgon is turned inward.

> Scapegoat-identified individuals are focused not on their own creative source but on defensive service to the ideals of the collective and on their own incapacity and rejectability. . . . The perfectionism of the inner scapegoating accuser clogs the improvisational play necessary for finding one's own voice. And while its high standards may aid in the acquisition of disciplined work habits, and may help one accomplish standardized or assigned chores, they are counterproductive for tasks requiring creativity, the expression of the originality of the individual self. (Perera 1986, 29)

Wurmser (1995) speaks of the heroic transcendence of shame through creativity. When one is gripped by the creative daimon, he suggests, "The boundaries between self and parts of the outside world, between various objects, between different feelings, moods, images, and memories melt away. A heightened sense of being alive, of attaining the best within, the ultimate meaning of oneself, even an increasing feeling of bodily vitality, is accompanied by a reaching out to others. . . . The creative experience is a form of love with strong narcissistic aspects" (293). "The most felicitous creativity,"

113

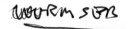

he adds, "may at least for a moment overcome that mortal woundedness in the core of the self . . . " (299).

My personal experience allows me to agree with him, as do the experiences of friends who tell me of their own feelings of release when they are pursuing activities which fully engage them. I recently watched on television a well-known, successful violinist whom I last saw in person when she was young and cut a very striking figure according to our culture's standards for youthful beauty. Today she has clearly moved into middle age and no longer has those dramatic looks, a "loss" made amply clear by the camera close-ups of her chin resting on the violin. Wrestling now and then with my problems (shame) around aging—from which few women escape in this culture—I took as an object lesson this brilliant musician's complete oblivion to everything but the music and her relationship to it. So fully engaged was her authentic self in its most meaningful expression that her dress might have come unsnapped, her hairdo been wildly mussed, and she would not have been in the least daunted.

Not all of us are "gripped" by genius as my violinist is, and too many discussions of creativity focus on the masters, the genius, setting standards for "the creative" that defeat rather than inspire. However, it is a rare individual who does not have some activity in which this same "gripping" and release occur—perhaps painting, writing, music, acting, but also perhaps gardening, sewing, carpentry, golf, riding a motorcycle. Once we identify that activity for ourselves, it is important, not to say imperative, to allow that activity as much time and space as possible *and* to focus on how we feel while we are in it so that we can begin to imagine what it would be like to feel that way in all our activities. For it is in these times that the ego is most disengaged from the wound and most engaged in relationship with the original self. By identifying and honoring this process, by learning to "transfer" its magic to other life activities, we add strength to the ego, bypass the wound of defilement and dread, give life to the original self, and make it possible to move into more and more life with less and less burden of shame.

Finally, Athene as emblem of wholeness consciously contains the opposites and knows how to walk "the middle way" between them, falling into neither one side nor the other. Admittedly, this is an almost godlike capacity, one to which we can perhaps only aspire. As Jung said, "Whoever can suffer within himself the highest united with the lowest is healed, holy, whole" (1973, 1: 365). For me, the operative word there is *united*, implying as it does the highest modality of psychological integration. Most of us spend our days being shunted from one polarity to another, experiencing the highest, then the lowest, our unconsciousness keeping us in a sort of psychological ping-pong match in which we are the ball. In some ways, the shamecarrier suffers this condition more acutely than others, because our dread of reiterating the catastrophe keeps us shackled to the collective's definition of "the highest" and makes embrace of "the lowest" anathema. To put it another way, shame and dread are not only the result of an essential disunion but are also impediments to achieving reunion. But our choice is spelled out in this passage from Jung:

> The one-after-another [of the opposites] is a bearable prelude to the deeper knowledge of the side-by-side, for this is an incomparably more difficult problem. Again, the view that good and evil are spiritual forces outside us, and that man is caught in the conflict between them, is more bearable by far than the insight that the opposites are the ineradicable and indispensable preconditions of all psychic life, so much so that life itself is guilt. (Jung 1963, 169-70)

It appears that we have a choice between continuing to be caught in the conflict or taking up our shadow work, going within to discover that "wholeness" means precisely that and is not always pretty: that to be whole means to acknowledge and be responsible for the darkness within as well as the light. The difficulty with that is that it means confronting our capacity for evil. But if we do not confront it, we cannot be responsible for its presence in us, nor can we hope to control its manifestations. Moreover, if we continue to locate the forces of evil and good outside ourselves, neither can we claim the good which is within. Unless we know the opposites and know that we contain them, we cannot possibly begin to discover how to walk the middle way.

Walking the middle way psychologically means that we are less subject to falling into one-sidedness. We are less subject to positive inflation ("I'm divine, . . . " a pitfall for the shamecarrier looking for compensation) and to negative inflation ("I'm ashes and dust, . . . " the shamecarrier's favorite slogan, which opens us up to every critical, abusing inner voice, derogates our value, reiterates the primal defilement, and generally causes us all kinds of trouble in the outer as well as the inner world). Walking the middle way means staying grounded in one's own values, being less manipulated by flattery, praise, or criticism. It means being able to choose right companions and activities. It means being able to honor what is valuable in the collective without sacrificing to it what is valuable about our selves. It means stopping to ask ourselves, "Does this action/opinion/concern, etc., feel more like *me* or like conformity to an introject or someone's expectation?" Perhaps more than anything else, walking the middle way means that we have evolved the strength to endure the tension of the opposites, which either work to pull us apart or to crush us in their collision.

Those of us who remain caught in the medical model of psychology (and most of us do, because it so permeates our culture), who half consciously continue to believe that psychological pain is always to be *cured* rather than understood and suffered, need to discard the idea that this "middle way," this "third place" is one of tranquillity and harmony. Instead, it is exactly that place where the opposites collide, and since the opposites never disappear but remain always potentially in collision, the "third place" will always be tensive. Wholeness, then, the conscious gathering together and acknowledgement of everything we are, many aspects of which are in opposition to one another, would seem to have more to do with strength, compassion, patience, and humility than they do with peace and harmony; more to do with the capacity to endure tension and find meaning in it than with its dissipation.

TURNING THE GORGON: A PSYCHOLOGICAL APPROACH

Since we have located the origins of dread in infancy, it follows that its psychological transformation must take place in the infantile part of the psyche. Moreover, since primordial dread and defilement became imprinted because of empathic failures in the early environment, it follows that what is needed now is an effort to repair the effects of those failures. We need to provide for our inner infant the holding environment which was absent during our actual infancy. "Work on what the mother has spoiled," to paraphrase the *I Ching*. While we cannot ever repair the past, which is gone forever and indelibly fixed, we can to some extent repair its effects, which continue in the living infant of the present.

Winnicott (1975, 159-60) provides a very clear outline of what the Good Mother does. The following, he says, are vitally important:

— She exists, continues to exist, lives, smells, breathes, her heart beats. She is *there* to be sensed in all possible ways.

— She loves in a physical way, provides contact, a body temperature, movement, and quiet according to the baby's needs.

— She provides opportunity for the baby to make the transition between the quiet and the excited state, not suddenly coming at the child with a feed and demanding response.

— She provides suitable food at suitable times.

— At first she lets the infant dominate, being willing (as the child is so nearly a part of herself) to hold herself in readiness to respond. Gradually she introduces the external shared world, carefully grading this according to the child's needs which vary from day to day and hour to hour.

— She protects the baby from coincidences and shocks (the door banging as the baby goes to the breast), trying to keep the physical and emotional situation simple enough for the infant to be able to understand, and yet rich enough according to the infant's growing capacity.

— She provides continuity.

— By believing in the infant as a human being in its own right she does not hurry his development and so enables him to catch hold of time, to get the feeling of an internal personal going along. For the mother the child is a whole human being from the start, and this enables her to tolerate his lack of integration and his weak sense of living-in-the-body.

One way to understand these guidelines in terms of how our adult self relates to the inner infant is to look at what we do that violates or ignores them, what we do that is not good mothering and replicates the shove back into chaos. Probably the first and absolutely fundamental way in which we fail empathically is that we do not acknowledge the infant's existence. Frankly, I don't know many people who do, and I was more than a decade in analysis before I did—not that my experience is predic-tive, by any means. As I mentioned in the foreword, I had for years worked with the concept of the "wounded child complex," but in my ignorance (and probably defensively) saw my "wounded child" as being six or seven years old. Somehow, that seemed acceptable to me, less shaming, but when I discovered that this wounded child was a wounded *infant*, I spent two or three days feeling shattered and humiliated. At *my* age? After all these years of analysis? Surely it meant that all my efforts to become more con-scious had achieved nothing. To make matters worse, just the knowledge that the infant was there seemed to work as a vortex sucking me close to the chaotic crater, the Deep Canyon, Ogden's catastrophe, and there were moments during this experience when I was not altogether certain I was not going to fragment. But I did not, and by the fourth day I began to feel a deep, quiet joy at the infant's presence, a sense of wholeness, an inarticulable, ineffable integration that had not been there before—or perhaps what I felt was the infant's joy at being "seen." In the ensuing weeks, I learned (to my relief) that the infantile psyche is present in ev-eryone, that it is a normality, not a pathology. Eventually, I was able to understand some of my past reactions and behaviors in a new and helpful way, and that ahead of me lay daily opportunities and responsibilities for making a conscious relationship with the infant.

One example of the effects of denying/ignoring the infant's existence will also serve as an example of a violation of Winnicott's "rule" about suit-able food at suitable times:

For more than two years, I had been remodeling a newly purchased home, often living in a chaos of plaster, sawdust, noise, interruptions, and the tendency of things such as eyeglasses, tools, cats, grocery lists to relocate and hide themselves. Wanting badly to achieve order, peace, and quiet, and wanting just as badly to avoid shame by making certain that I was carrying my fair share of the workload, I kept deferring the "food" which was not only suitable but had become imperative: quiet hours of reading, drawing, musing, relating to my inner life, and giving myself over to primary process thought. One morning of the twenty-third month of this, I went to open a sliding screen door only to find that it was so recalcitrant it might as well have been nailed down and glued. In that instant, a rage rose up in me which would have made Charles Manson look like Patient Griselda. It was berserker rage, and had I identified with it (which I came within an ace of doing), I would have ripped the screen off its tracks with my bare hands and smashed everything within a wide radius. But a few seconds into this affect, I felt its nature, that it was the archaic, primitive rage of the infant at not being fed, not being given the suitable food of tranquillity, of being able, as Winnicott says, to continue "going on being," of having time for spontaneity, self-expression, play.

If we do not acknowledge the infant's existence, we cannot know what its needs are. Not to be in relationship to the inner baby is the equivalent of the physical mother who does not provide the loving physical contact mentioned in Winnicott's second guideline for good mothering. We know by now that infants who are not held and touched by their mothers can stop living within a few weeks; imagine the torment of the inner infant who exists in a state of neglect, abandonment, abuse for decades.

We violate the precepts of what constitutes a good mother when we allow what the Freudians call the superego—or any other element of the psyche—to override the needs of the infant self, which is for all present purposes the original self. We violate them when we reiterate the threat of annihilation, which we do every time we upbraid ourselves for having been spontaneous and free, for showing our real feelings, for expressing an opinion or sharing an idea, for not having a certain dress or job or college degree, and so on—every time the ego identifies with the corrosive, soul-killing inner voice. Very often that voice belongs to the distorted inner mother or father image, who is probably aping something we heard as a child, or thought we heard, from an outer parent. Robert Stein gives us an apt general description of the messages from the distorted inner parent:

> Fundamentally, the negative parent archetype manifests itself by being persistently dissatisfied with the way one is, never accepting the uniqueness, the strengths and limitations of one's being. It thrives by holding up images and concepts of how and where one should be. Whenever life begins to flow it attempts to hold it back by provoking guilt and fear, and by rejecting the validity of the subjective personal experience. It causes us to neglect the basic needs and desires of our souls by labeling them as childish, immature, false, destructive or inconsequential. In place of the soul's authentic needs, it provokes us to pursue some hollow image of spiritual perfection. Whenever a real flame of love and passion begins to burn brightly, it screams

hysterical warnings of doom and disaster. It loses its wits completely whenever the rational mind is on the verge of surrendering to a greater unknown power. (Stein 1973, 178)

Ego identification with the wide variety of psychic elements also dissipates the ego function and gives it a constantly shifting coloration. That is, if the ego "becomes" the lover, then the victim, then the parent, then the child, then the wise old man or woman, then the artist, then the hero, the all-giving mother, the witch, etc., beyond a certain point there is no ego there at all, no stable center of consciousness, and this violates Winnicott's "rule" that the mother must provide continuity.

In some ways one of the most difficult of Winnicott's precepts, specially for those of us in the demanding Western collective, is the need to let the infant dominate. Most of us don't know how to do this appropriately, and as a result we find ourselves overtaken by eruptions of infantile affects and behaviors, which can range from "unexplained" fears of abandonment and weeping to the violence of physical abuse or worse. A good model for appropriate ways and times to let the infant dominate (and an example of reclaiming the chthonic values) was provided by Jung, who, recognizing the deep need of his inner child to escape from the pressures of Jung's profession, periodically spent hours at the lake shore, making canals and dams in the mud and sailing toy boats. I find it touching that this massive, evolved intelligence could also be so profoundly simple and direct. An important point here is that, as with Jung, we do not *abandon* the ego to the infant, which we do when we identify with its affects; instead, the infant must be allowed to dominate *with the assent, in the presence of, and in relationship to the ego*. The interior psychological picture is exactly analogous to the outer picture of a mother watching over her baby as it plays, providing a loving presence, participating in the activity in appropriate ways, and keeping an unobtrusive eye on concerns of safety and limits.

In his sensitive, empathic study of shame, Léon Wurmser makes this observation:

Shame's aim is disappearance. This may be, most simply, in the form of hiding; most radically in the form of dissolution (suicide); most mythically, in the form of change into another shape; . . . most archaically in the form of freezing into complete paralysis and stupor;

most frequently, in the form of forgetting parts of one's life and one's self; and at its most differentiated, in the form of changing one's character. (Wurmser 1995, 84)

Much as I find to admire in this statement, I have trouble agreeing with its last phrase—assuming, of course, that I correctly understand what its author means by "one's character." Taken at face value and in the context of Wurmser's assertion that shame is caused by a belief that one is essentially unloveable, the phrase implies that the reason one is unloveable is that something is wrong with one's character to begin with and that if we change it we may become loveable. This argument keeps the shamecarrier on the same old wheel of trying to be something or someone else; it perpetuates the compensations, the defenses, the reaching for perfection, the self-devaluation, and the dread of annihilation because one fails, does not deserve to exist. I would take the liberty of revising the last phrase to read "at its most differentiated, in the form of *changing the character of one's relationship to the original self.*" In achieving that, we do not disappear, we *appear* for the first time as who we are. Part of our work to move us in the direction of this achievement consists in creating the empathic good-mother environment and in coming into a right relationship with our inner infant. Through this work, we reiterate Athene's act which restores the Gorgon to her original status as healing protector; that is, we use dread and shame as symbols rather than as dis-eases—as symbolizing affects containing a constant impulse aiming towards something beyond what they express, as Vernant said: in our case, aiming toward the origin of the affect. Behind it lies the gold of the original, unconditioned, undefiled self.

TURNING THE GORGON: A SPIRITUAL APPROACH

In *The Future of an Illusion*, Freud made this very provocative statement about the relationship of the human to the divine:

Critics persist in calling "deeply religious" a person who confesses to a sense of man's insignificance and impotence in face of the universe, although it is not this feeling that constitutes the essence of religious emotion, but rather the next step, the reaction to it, which seeks a remedy against this feeling. He who goes no further, he who humbly acquiesces in the insignificant part man plays in the universe, is, on the contrary, irreligious in the truest sense of the word. (Freud n.d., 56-7; Robson-Scott trans.)

This was written almost seventy years ago, decades during which the rabid profiteering from and devastation of the earth because of Western man's arrogant inflation—his overstatement of his significance—is good reason to take some issue with Freud's view. We could do with some humble ac-quiescence from a technological and corporate collective that from the evidence has neither shame nor reverence.

Nonetheless, Freud's thought catches a signal relevance for the indi-vidual struggling to erect a sense of significance out of the burning swamp of defilement, shame, and dread. It underscores what is, beneath the many important psychological issues, the ultimate but often neglected issue for the shamecarrier, the issue of our relationship to the transcendent. "The decisive question for man," wrote Jung, "is: Is he related to something infi-nite or not?"

That is the telling question of his life. . . . If we understand and feel that here in this life we already have a link with the infinite, desires and attitudes change. In the final analysis, we count for something only because of the essential we embody, and if we do not embody that, life is wasted. (Jung 1961, 325)

For the shamecarrier, what is absent from this embodiment and from the relationship to the divine is *aidos* in Democritus' sense: reverence for self. In that simple phrase much is implied: recognition that we are a unique and valuable creation of the divine; that we know we have value *by virtue of our existence* without regard to performance or social standing; that we are therefore aware of our inherent dignity. It is this sense of *aidos* which ac-cords us our greatest possibility for recognizing the majesty inherent in the human condition. As Wurmser says, "It is characteristic of the tragic hero that he transcends his shame by what Sophocles repeatedly called nobility" (1995, 293). This nobility, majesty, sense of dignity enables us to endure suffering, the tension between the opposites, deprivation and loss, all the ills which attend our human status, including our sometime sense of being burdened by our own selves and the darkness of our shadow. Sometimes it may be our only source of support in facing the reality of the dark side of the Holy, the *tremendum,* the Wrath of god, which can manifest as the threat of psychological as well as physical catastrophe.

Somewhat paradoxically, it is also *aidos* that opens the door to compassion for self, because conscious, informed reverence for self also implies acceptance of the limitations inherent in being human. (Nobility is never at issue if one is omnipotent.) Fully to know and accept our station midway between nothing-ness and the divine is to know and accept that we are powerful but only up to a point; significant but only in a circumscribed way; competent but only within limits; that our finite minds cannot penetrate infinitude; that "perfection" is out of reach; that errors, projections, inflations, ignorance are inevitable; that our physical self is, after all, biodegradable . . . and out of that awareness to come not to self-contempt and abjectness (which Ricoeur suggests are "substi-tuted for the humble confession of the sinner," (1967, 145), but to a loving compassion for self, that we must live strung across the abyss between damna-tion and perfection. "How far can our love extend," asks Hillman, "to the broken and ruined parts of ourselves, the disgusting and perverse?"

> How much charity and compassion have we for our own weakness and sickness? How far can we build an inner society on the principle of love, allowing a place for everyone? . . . Loving oneself is no easy matter just because it means loving all of oneself, including the shadow where one is inferior and socially so unacceptable. The care one gives this humiliating part is also the cure. (Hillman 1967, 75-6)

Seeing our condition and admitting compassion among our responses, it follows that we will better be able to recognize the same condition in other humans and in other life forms. Then those who inhabit the earth with us will be less likely to become targets for projections of contempt, more likely to be recipients of understanding. This has the additional effect of making it more difficult to place the other, whether friend, lover, employer, pastor, *in loco Dei,* relieving them of the power to produce shame in us, and of the intolerable burden of responsibility for our well-being. It also mitigates shame's power to isolate and alienate. Transforming the Gorgon allows the Eros bridge to the outer world to be restored.

Yet another effect of feeling *aidos* for oneself is that it helps to break what psychoanalysis has seen as the Eros-Thanatos conflict, in which the "life or love instinct is permanently threatened by [the] death instinct (aggression, destructiveness, hate and envy)" (Guntrip 1973, 66-7). Self-*aidos* enables us to enter life more fully and to engage in it with a more spontaneous, authentic self. In the overview of the literature, we saw that a dominant aspect of shame is that it is life-denying; the ensuing text periodically underscored that the inevitable counterpart of that is to be death-oriented. If the creative (which is life-oriented and life-affirming) is "gripping," as Wurmser puts it, so is the destructive, of which shame is one modality. The shame affect can be seen as a form of possession no less than the affects, positive or negative, of falling in love, being taken over by the creative daimon, or falling into the negative animus or any other of the archetypes. But to be gripped by the creative is to be drawn into more life: at some point in the creative process, libido and expression flow outward, bringing about a poem, an orchid, a new dress, a richer relationship. To be gripped by shame is to be drawn towards non-life, some form of death; it swamps the ego and contracts it inward, as though we were being sucked down in a horrid vortex to a place of not-being. Dread, we could say, is the fear of that possession. It is not uncommon for people caught in the life-death conflict to strengthen *aidos* by making, even if they have to force it, a conscious choice between the opposites of life and death. The negative Gorgon's idea of death can be quite seductive, and her first action is to petrify—to make life energy unavailable to the ego. Fighting that petrifaction is an act of ethical courage, and there are times when it means making over and over again the choice for life, sometimes for no other reason than that one has made the commitment to do so—the commitment to "embody the essential link with the infinite," even if we are not yet quite sure what that means in a concrete, specific way.

Finally, it is possible to transform the Gorgon by learning to understand shame and dread as the *felix culpa*, the "happy fault" because of which we may be led to see the potential of unity of self and reunion of self with the divine—in Neumann's terms, of restoring the ego-self axis. Just as the sense of one's creaturely defilement and nullity are "the numinous raw material for the feeling of religious humility" (Otto 1958, 19), the affects of shame and dread serve to make us aware and can become the raw material of growth. They are too strong to be ignored, and even if we manage to ignore them for a time, we do so at great risk to the economy and health of our psyche. To "pathologizings" such as shame, James Hillman says, we owe a great debt.

> Pathologizing . . . breaks the soul free from its identification with ego and its life and the upperworld heroes of light and high gods who provide the ego with its models, and who have cast our consciousness in a one-sided, suppressive narrowness regarding life, health, and nature. Symptoms, not therapists, led this century to soul. . . . We owe our symptoms a great debt. The soul can exist without its therapists, but not without its afflictions. (Hillman 1975, 71)

Explicating the Adamic myth and god's regard of human sin, Ricoeur writes:

> If the principal emphasis is not placed on the degrading character of the situation of being-seen-by god, it is because the primordial significance of this seeing is to constitute the *truth* of my situation, the justness and the justice of the ethical judgment that can be passed on my existence. That is why this seeing, far from preventing the birth of the Self, gives rise to self-awareness; it enters into the field of subjectivity as the *task* of knowing oneself better; this seeing, which *is*, lays the foundation for the ought-to-be of self awareness. (Ricoeur 1967, 84-5)

To paraphrase an old saw, the wound becomes the window to the soul. Without the affects, our unconsciousness would continue and we would be deprived of the opportunity to grow, to live more fully, more authentically, more responsibly.

For this reason, shame and dread, although experienced as painful psychological chaos, are, if worked through, opportunities to establish order by integrating into consciousness elements of our lives which were both unconscious and critically important. Again I refer to Ricoeur's work precisely because he is not a psychologist but validates a psychological dynamic with fresh language from another discipline.

> Along with the dread of being stricken, annihilated, there is perception of the movement by which order . . . is restored. That which had been

125

established and which has now been destroyed is re-established. By negation, order reaffirms itself. (Ricoeur 1967, 43)

This reminds us once more of the truism that whenever something is made conscious, something else must be destroyed—here, the unconsciousness surrounding the roots of shame and, at least to some degree, the autonomous potency of its affect.

These shifts in the psyche are analogous to redemption in the Christian sense, pointing as they do to a change in the ego from its adaptive, conditioned form to one closer to the form originally intended by the Creator. The ego is, we might say, redeemed of the sin of which Carotenuto wrote, the sin against oneself when we do not live as we really are. It is the once-prodigal, able now to reconnect with the Self which from infancy had been perceived as hostile and negative.

Some of the most important implications of the ego's relationship to the Self are explored in this, from Edinger:

> The process of becoming conscious requires both seeing and being seen, knowing and being known. This is not hard to understand from the standpoint of the ego; but if there is to be true withness in our knowing, the same must apply to the other center of the process, namely the Self. The Self must also need to be known as well as to know. . . . The pursuit of consciousness, then, does not allow one to rest in the attitude of being known and contained in god; *the ego has a responsibility to the Self to be its knowing subject as well as its known object.* (Edinger 1984, 53)

It is this understanding of the relationship between the ego and the Self which causes analytical psychology to assert that consciousness is a moral and religious issue, that caused Jung to state, "As far as we can discern, the sole purpose of human existence is to kindle a light in the darkness of mere being. It may even be assumed that just as the unconscious affects us, so the increase in our consciousness affects the unconscious" (Jung 1961, 326). And it is this understanding of the ego's position in the psychic structure—as the known object of the Self—that leads analytical psychology to the position that it is not always "cure" which is sought but the meaning of our suffering; a pathology may not be healed, but if its meaning can be understood in the transpersonal context, the condition can then be endured.

To stay with the Judaeo-Christian metaphor, we might also say that the negatively-perceived Self is analogous to what Ricoeur calls the misunderstood Wrath of god, which is really "only the sadness of love" (Ricoeur 1967, 67). For our purposes now, the sadness of the Self at the prodigality and consequent suffering of the defensive, adaptive ego. This state of affairs can, of course, continue to the end of life; one can either suffer neurotically, as Jung said, or *meaningfully*. That may not seem like much of a choice if one's goal is simply to be extricated from suffering altogether, but the difference between the two options lies in embodying or not embodying the essential, having or not having a link with the infinite. Our only real options are to live our neurosis or our life. Ricoeur once more:

> Salvation, in the tragic vision, is not outside the tragic but within it. This is the meaning of . . . that "suffering for the sake of understanding" which is celebrated by the chorus in Aeschylus' *Agamemnon*: " . . . I have pondered all; I recognize only Zeus as he who can relieve me of the burden of my sterile anguish. . . . He has opened up to men the ways of prudence, giving them the law *of suffering for the sake of understanding*. When in sleep, in the sight of the heart, painful remorse descends, wisdom enters into them in spite of themselves. And that, I think, is the benevolent violence of the gods, seated at the bar of heaven" (*Ag.*, 160*ff*). "Suffering for the sake of understanding"—that is tragic wisdom, that is "tragic knowledge," to speak like Karl Jaspers. (Ibid., 229)

A very nice distinction between meaningful and neurotic suffering is made by Helen Luke, who points out that our "suffer" derives from Latin *ferre*, meaning "to bear," plus "sub," meaning "under." Suffering, then, carries the sense of bearing the weight and implies an upward thrust. In contrast, "such terms as 'affliction,' 'grief,' and 'depression' all bring images of weight bearing *down*."

> There are, then, two kinds of experiences which we call suffering—that which is totally unproductive, the neurotic state of meaningless depression, and that which is the essential condition of every step on the way to what C. G. Jung has called individuation. Perhaps these

images of weight under which we fall and lie in self-pity, or of weight which we carry in full consciousness, may be a guideline in moments of darkness. . . . Every time a person exchanges neurotic depression for real suffering, he or she is sharing to some small degree in the carrying of the suffering of mankind, in bearing a tiny part of the darkness of the world. Such a one is released from his small personal concern into a sense of *meaning*. (Luke 1987, 103-7)

The many aspects of the very demanding work which ontic shame sets before us, as well as the hazards and rewards which follow that work, are summed up in Thomas van Nortwick's words about Greek culture: "The message it sends to us is simple enough to understand, if hard to accept: to be a hero is finally to embrace the person we really are, and to live in the world that this acceptance creates all around us" (1992, 184).

It would be a mistake to read his thought too heroically, failing to hear its cautionary note. Our acceptance of ourselves does not always create a world of friendly joy; the world may greet our growth with indifference, disappointment, or even with hostility, since the collective also has its negative Gorgon aspect which would freeze us in place. It does take courage to be who we are, but the embrace of the collective is a poor thing compared to the certain knowledge that we have the right to exist, just as we are. "The theological equivalent to this experience," Edinger says, "is justification before god" (1974, 167).

Before what kind of god do we justify ourselves? This fundamental question, one which underlies the entire field of the shame issue, I have left for the last of our meditation together. Have we arrived at our personal perception of the divine? What is that perception—have we denied the *tremendum* aspect altogether? Or are we captive of it, in our captivity denied sight of the other faces of the holy: the *augustum*, for example, or the face of love? Do we admit wholeness to our concept: is "god" entirely masculine, or is one face of the holy a feminine face, perhaps Athene's, in which we may, like the old Greeks, find "joy, help, and salvation?"

The centrality of the search for answers to these and similar questions was made abundantly clear by Jung in a 1945 letter:

The main interest of my work is not concerned with the treatment of neuroses but rather with the approach to the numinous. But the fact is that the approach to the numinous is the real therapy and inasmuch as you attain to the numinous experience, you are released from the curse of pathology.

Citing this passage, Marie-Louise von Franz comments that it "says everything of essential importance about a Jungian analysis. If it is not possible to establish a relationship with the numinous, no cure is possible; the most one can hope for is an improvement in social adjustment" (1993, 177).

Here the fundamental question for the shamecarrier is how to find a positive relationship to the numinous when the numinous has been experienced with dread, as hostile, wrathful, potentially annihilating. In psychological terms, how do we restore relationship with the self when the self is not experienced by the ego as a positive. In religious terms, how do we begin to see the divine face of love more often than the face of wrath?

Von Franz answers that preconceived ideas and other impediments to the experience of the numinous must be removed. "The religious dimension in analysis," she writes, "is nothing other than finding new meaning in just this way that sometimes brings already existing religious ideas back to life, and sometimes transforms them" (ibid., 183). But the work also means "a struggle with the dark side of god (or the self), which the human being cannot face but must, as Job did" (ibid., 195).

> In the religious image of the deity, that is, the Self, the opposites coexist; however, they are not consciously unified. That can only occur in conscious people in whom both sides of the Self, the good and the evil, are working towards incarnation. In the incarnated form both sides are diminished and humanized and thus, through the agency of human consciousness, are able to enter into connection. Self-knowledge, or the development of consciousness, is thus the key factor. (Ibid., 197)

Paradoxically—and it is a paradox which also runs through all the major religious traditions—the ego must be the strong, flexible instrument of consciousness, the "eye" in the world, and at the same time must acknowledge its position as *subject* of the Self. As von Franz says, the *vox dei* can be heard only when the ego, "with all its opinions, pro and con, has died upon the cross" (ibid., 184).

The answer of the Western church would not differ significantly from von Franz' answer. Let us look at some passages from the writings of Thomas Merton, if not the only Christian mystic of Twentieth-Century America, probably the best known. There are aspects of his work which are difficult for me, most notably his exclusive use of the masculine gender in reference to the holy—just as there are elements in this book with which he would probably be unable to agree—but his lifetime of contemplating and experiencing the divine produced a body of work unique in American religious thought, one which can serve as a wise, compassionate guide for non-Christian and Christian alike. In psychology, he appears to have known most about Freud, but many of his observations are strikingly Jungian. For example:

> If I never become what I am meant to be, but always remain what I am not, I shall spend eternity contradicting myself by being at once something and nothing, a life that wants to live and is dead, a death that wants to be dead and cannot quite achieve its own death because it still has to exist. (1972, 33)

> The object of salvation is that which is unique, irreplaceable, incommunicable—that which is myself alone. This true inner self must be drawn up like a jewel from the bottom of the sea, rescued from confusion, from indistinction, from immersion in the common, the nondescript, the trivial, the sordid, the evanescent. (Ibid., 38)

Only when the superficial self—psychologically, the adapted ego—is set aside, or at least understands the extent of its falseness, can the true self be glimpsed, and it is the true self which is able to see the face of numinous love. "The only true joy on earth," Merton writes, "is to escape from the prison of our own false self, and enter by love into union with the Life who dwells and sings within the essence of every creature and in the core of our own souls" (ibid., 25). For Merton, grounded in Christian mysticism, it is the perversity and willfulness (might he have said "woundedness"?) of the false self which sees wrath in the face of the divine, just as for Neumann it is the distress ego which sees the Self as hostile.

For any of us, but specially for those of us who have been lifelong carriers of shame and dread, what Merton describes as entry into union with Life is a specific and ultimate grace, a freedom so nearly unimaginable that it seems magical. It is a form of magic both Athene and the Gorgon would understand, for it effects, as did their powers, an essential transformation of reality. In the antiquity of their origins, "magic" meant the same thing as *tekhne*: knowing how. Knowing how, in the heart as well as in the mind, is all we need—along with desire and, from time to time, a little dispensation from the gods.

Afterword

Coming to the end of this meditation, I am keenly aware of its "overflow," of the many questions I have not pursued, the roads not taken which could profitably have been taken but which lead to states and nations too large to be explored here. I have not pursued, for example, the relationship between defilement and the concept of original sin—the idea that humans are innately flawed—or Jung's assertion that dualism is inherent in the psyche and how that would play into formations of concepts of the divine, or the nature of evil. . . . These and other issues, unmistakably relevant to shame, may have occurred to the reader making his or her way through this text, and perhaps she or he will pursue them through other studies. Or perhaps they are all best worked out in the privacy of the heart.

Two contents of that "overflow," however, I do not want to leave unsaid. One is the imperative of "transforming the Gorgon" which hides in each of us—imperative because we are seeing in the world today the brutal results of the untransformed Gorgon working her rage upon the earth, upon animals, upon humans, upon life itself through the agency of individuals who have not taken the responsibility to create more consciousness. Our solitary personal work, which may sometimes seen negligible because we are only one person, is perhaps not the only antidote to this global poison, but it is a critically important one.

The second content which has been with me throughout the writing but one which I could not gracefully work into the main text is the image of Teiresias, which has appeared repeatedly, insisting that it is an apt emblem for the responsible shamecarrier. The reader will recall that Teiresias, in one myth form, violated Athene's privacy during her bath (like the un-initiated, unprepared infant, he saw what he was not supposed to see). For this transgression, and by the law of the gods, he was blinded. But Athene, to compensate him for his grave loss, gave him the gifts of divination, long life, and the strength to keep his wits about him in the Underworld. Just so, we who are blinded by shame and dread because we saw too much when we were uninitiated may be blessed by the goddess with the compensatory gifts of divination—of an intuition of health and wholeness—and of strength of mind which will keep us from falling into the psychotic catastrophe. Being diviners, we may be able to let the benevolence of that gift flow out to others as well as inward to our selves.

Appendix to Chapter Two

Note: The reader will find that I have not inserted "B. C." after dates, since it is understood that year notations always refer to the time before the Western demarcation of the birth of Christ. To avoid any possible confusion, I have, however, appended "A. D." to the few dates where that was necessary. Additionally, I have chosen in most cases to use the name spellings which come closest to the Greek in transliteration—e.g., Akhilleus instead of Achilles—out of respect for the sanctity of the earlier language and to expunge the now commonplace Latinized forms into which the Greek names fell under the Romans. I hope the reader will agree with me that the use of these less customary spellings helps to scale away the encrustations of stereotypes and to bring a fresh brightness to the persons of Greek myth. I have also eliminated diacritical marks; scholars of old Greek state that such marks are a late addition and did not exist in the original language.

The statements of some major scholars (e.g., Nilsson 1927/1949, Harrison 1903/1991, Dodds 1951, Parker 1989) to the effect that Athene was a pre-Greek goddess bearing strong resemblance to the house goddess of the Minoan culture (ca. 3000-1600) pointed the direction for my search for the pre-patriarchal Athene. The main path of that search took on the following general configuration: (1) Athene's origins as the Minoan house guardian, or Snake goddess—for which there is considerable iconographic evidence, specially in snake imagery so frequently connected with Athene—places her origin in a religion which is essentially matriarchal, a religion of the goddess, and in a culture characterized as peace-loving, exuberant, reverential of life in all its forms.

135

The implications these parameters carry for the early nature of "Athene" are clear. (2) The Minoan civilization was eclipsed by northern people who came to be known as the Mycenaeans. Perceptive enough to see the cultural superiority of the Minoan culture over their own, the Mycenaeans assimilated many of its aspects, including the goddess-dominated religion—to which, however, they added their own male gods. Among the pantheon of the Mycenaeans was a goddess named "Athana" or "Atana," often assumed to be a variant or early name for Athene. From other evidence it is known that the Mycenaeans retained the "house guardian," who in their culture became the palace guardian attached to the king, who was high priest as well as political leader. Unlike the Minoans, the Mycenaeans were warlike, frequently engaged in battle, and it follows that the "palace guardian" would accompany the king-priest into battle, to protect him and his men. I believe we see here the origin of the idea of Athene as "battle maiden," but she still retained her central aspect as maternal guardian of the family and the well-being of the race. (3) The Mycenaean culture was virtually destroyed ca. 1100 by marauding tribes from the north, who replaced the palace culture with a quasi-political organization based on the family unit with the father as the supreme authority. This wholly male-dominated organization became the model for a revised and patriarchal pantheon, probably with Zeus at the helm. During this "Dark Age," about which almost nothing is known, poverty, illiteracy, chaos, and primitivity reigned. The matriarchal tendencies of the old religious order were suppressed. (4) The utterly patriarchal world view and cosmology were inherited by the archaic age (ca. 750-480), during which honor, justice, order, and pure reason were invested with supreme value. Athene, who makes her first recorded appearance in the *Iliad*, retains her role as guardian, and now must "officially" be the guardian of the state and its constructs—which is to say, she is made the handmaiden of the collective and is given yet another title, "goddess of Reason," to reflect the new values. By the classical period (ca. 480-380), she is almost completely "partiarchalized," if I may be forgiven such a word, and has assumed the delineations which have made up the common view of her from Hellenistic times into our own era.

In addition to these historical reasons, I am persuaded of Athene's pre-patriarchal and pre-Greek origins by the proliferation of stories of her birth. She is variously said to have been sired by Zeus and sprung from his forehead (sometimes his beard)—the version we know best; to have been sired by Poseidon, by one of the primordial Giants, or Titans (Pallas), by one of the Kyklopes, by one of the *daktyloi*, by the river-god Triton. When there are so many myths and tales about a subject, it is unreasonable to give all credence to a single one, specially if it is the youngest, as the Zeus-forehead myth appears to be. Not only is it probably the most recent, but its symbolic action coincides with suspicious neatness with the archaic and classical valuation of rationality and order. I am inclined to accept without reservation Kerényi's assertion about her birth largely because it embraces antiquity, the archetypal understanding of the Great Mother, and the archetypal nature of pan-cultural myths about the autochthonous genesis of so many deities. Moreover, it fits with the many connections of Athene with Poseidon, her associations with the invention of the ship, and several other motifs. Here is what Kerényi says: "The surname Tritogeneia [which appears in Homer and elsewhere] did not originally mean that she came into the world on the banks of any particular river or lake, but that *she was born of the water itself*; for the name Triton seems to be associated with water generally" (1951, 128; emphasis mine). H. J. Rose would concur: "Her cult is commonly found connected with a stream or body of water of some kind, from the little river Triton near Aliphera in Arkadia . . . to Lake Tritonis in Africa, in which continent she was identified with native goddesses" (1991, 108-9). (Graves [1959, 1: 148] cites Skylax for the information that in classical times Lake Tritonis still covered nine hundred square miles. It is now the salt marshes of Chott Melghir and Chott ed Jerid in Libya.)

Could this be why Athene, as some writers have observed, never acknowledged her mother—that is, never acknowledged Metis, the "mother" supplied by the Zeus-forehead Olympian myth. "Metis" means reflection, or good counsel, but also, sometimes, cunning, and in all likelihood her assignment as Athene's mother began during the archaic period, which first formed the habit of personifying abstract concepts such as Justice, Abundance, etc.—a habit which served very well in the classical age with its love of philosophy, rationality, and precision of thought. Jaeger notes that Hesiod, in whose *Theogony* we first run into the idea that Metis was Athene's mother, "freely introduces fresh personifications to satisfy the new urge to abstract thinking" (1945, 1:65-6). Moreover, Burkert (1985) comments that abstract concepts became personified partly "because of the grammatical gender of abstract nouns" (184); the grammar to which he refers can only be the grammar of the first truly Greek language, which was not created until the mid-archaic period.

Virtually every scholar who writes of Athene, the venerable Martin Nilsson among them, describes her as a pre-Greek goddess with marked resemblance to the Minoan house goddess. From what can be told of the Minoans from the surviving art, architecture, and artifacts, they were a seafaring people of peaceful disposition. The tranquillity of their life can be construed from the absence of fortifications and by the rarity of depictions of war in their art. Exuberant and naturalistic, Minoan art is typically described as joyful, playful, spontaneous, inventive, keenly observant of life whether in humans, insects, plants, animals. Adam Hopkins writes, "In Cretan art . . . there is a total absence of the pomp and savagery found so commonly in other civilizations of the same era. This absence, together with the choice of undefended coastal sites for cities, is perhaps the most telling indication we possess of the whole tenor of Minoan society" (1977, 46).

Since Athene's origins have been located in this society, it is important to know that the Minoan religion was primarily a religion of the goddess. Frescoes depict women participating in the same events as men and as priestesses central to Minoan ritual, and excavations have unearthed many female "idols" but comparatively few male ones. The central point, of course, is that to be a house goddess in this culture was not a subordinate or inferior position; this was the function of one of the three primary feminine deities of the Minoan religion, the Snake goddess. (The other two were a Mistress of the Animals, who would develop into Artemis; and an anthropomorphic goddess which emerged from a tree cult.)

The sacred animals of the Minoan goddess were the snake and the bird. Both are among Athene's ancient emblems and were attached to her in sculpture of the archaic and even of the classical period. The bird was a common image of the goddess' epiphany, as it was for all the Minoan and later the Mycenaean deities. The bird motif is one which proliferates both in depictions of Athene and in her titles (e.g., Athene Aithyia, "sea-bird" or "diver-bird"). The bird we usually connect with Athene is the owl, but this has recently been said to be a late linkage probably originating in the wars with Persia, when the Greeks were convinced that Athene appeared to them on the battlefield in the form of an owl. There is no owl in Homer; instead, when Athene takes on animal form, it is always as a bird but never as an owl. Peter Levi (in Pausanias 1971, 1, 44, n. 84) argues that the word which in the *Iliad* is often translated as "grey" (*glaukopis*) can also be translated as "owl-faced," but Homer's consistent and repeated color-link of Athene's eyes with the sea and the absence of the owl image argue against Levi's assertion.

Athene's many appearances with snakes and birds tie her imagetically and symbolically to a genesis in the old Minoan religion. From what is known of this culture, certain things can be deduced about the nature of the Minoan "Athene." That she was profoundly linked with nature we can be sure. Her role as house guardian in the peaceful Minoan culture be-speaks a domestic familiarity and a concern for the welfare of the human family, therefore with human relationships—concerns which evince a ma-ternal interest more than they do the interests of a warrior. These, in turn, point to her connection with the agricultural and a focus on success in harvest and trade, more than in battle, at a time when food was the key to survival and agriculture was still largely woman's work. Emily Vermeule suggests that the "treasures" to be guarded were not gold or weapons or booty of war but farm products (1972, 37).

Sometime around 1600, a warlike tribe we designate as Mycenaeans (after their dominant stronghold, Mycenae) and which Homer called the Achaeans, subordinated but also assimilated the Minoan culture and came to flourish in the Late Bronze Age, ca. 1400-1200. The religion, the art, and much of the mythology of this culture had their roots in the Minoan culture, a blending which persisted until the demise of the Mycenaean civi-lization ca. 1100. Here, in this blended culture, were the origins of what became Greek mythology, of epic poetry, of the monumentality of classical Greek sculpture and architecture. Often building literally on Minoan sites, the Mycenaeans built as well on the Minoan religion, retaining the sym-bolic horns of consecration and the double axe (*labrys*), but more importantly the cults with which those symbols are associated, including that of the house goddess—eventually joined by their own male deity from the north.

While the lower classes sustained their belief in the chthonian nature deities, some of whom eventually ascended to Olympos, the upper class restructured the Mycenaean cosmology along the lines of their political pattern, which was feudal in nature. Thus their feudal organization, with the king at its head, later became the model for the State of the gods. In fact, the Mycenaean king, the *wanax*, was more than a political and mili-tary leader; he was also the high priest of the religion, and as Nilsson points out, "we must suppose that the Mycenaean king carried on the cult of the gods in his palace sanctuary. The gods and the cults of the king were the gods and the cults of the state" (1949, 487). The house goddess of the king was his protectress and was part of the patrimony inherited by the king's sons. Being attached to the king, she became attached as well to the place of which he was sovereign. Like the principal deity of the Minoans, she was called "Lady" (*potnia*) and because she protected the king, who was warlike, she accompanied him as he marched into battle.

This function of the house goddess, it could be argued, accounts for the appearance of a figure unearthed at Mycenae which archaeologists have dubbed "the Shield goddess." "A very curious figure is the Shield goddess . . . painted in the form of a large 8-shaped shield from behind which feet, hands, and a head project. Now near the same sanctuary a fresco of a goddess wearing a boar's tusk helmet has been found" (Burkert 1985, 42). There is no reason to discard the idea that this figure may have been an early image of Athene. There is a compelling if remote possibility that the Shield goddess from Mycenae is in fact a vestige of a much earlier image from the Neolithic period, in which woman and toad are combined to make a strikingly similar image. This hybrid, which seems to us rather bizarre, loses some of its strangeness in light of the fact that both participate symbolically in the idea of water as the origin of life.

Around 1000 the major centers of this empire were almost all destroyed, many by fire and probably by immigrant tribes from the north. Among those centers was Pylos, where, in the 1930s, Bronze Age tablets were discovered—ironically, fired hard and thus preserved by the very fire which destroyed the palace. These were incised with what came to be called Linear B script—what remained, along with other tablets found at Knossos, of the Mycenaean language. Deciphered by Michael Ventris in 1952, most of the tablets proved to be inventories, mostly of chariots, weapons, and food. But among them was one tablet, possibly recording a prayer, which preserved the names of Mycenaean deities, among them "Atana," or "Athana," often held to be a reference to Athene.

With the destruction of the Mycenaean culture, the country was plunged into the Dark Age, ca. 1100 to 750, a period referred to consistently as bleak, hard, and poverty-stricken. Virtually everything of the previous highly advanced civilization was swept aside, utterly demolished. Gone are the written language, any record of religion, the political structure. What had been a palace culture based on kingship was now a groping towards a new feudalism. Walter Burkert: "The collapse . . . about 1200 caused Greece and Crete to revert for more than 400 years to illiteracy and so to a prehistoric level. The sparseness of material remains makes these centuries dark in a further sense. All large-scale stone building ceased, as did the pictorial and plastic arts; even simple clay figures disappear for a time" (1985, 47). George Forrest speaks of the period as one of "chaotic tribal wandering" (1989, 14). We can imagine that people in such conditions would place little value on literacy, the arts, diplomacy—that it was a time when only brute male force guaranteed survival and a maternal deity was cast out in favor of a cosmology which reflected the tenor of the social environment. Now the father, not the king, was the supreme authority, a family structure which became the model for the Olympian family of gods, with Zeus as the father-ruler, the patriarch. What was by comparison to the Mycenaean era a cultural vacuum became the crucible for the formation of the patriarchal world view and the domination of the Father principle. With the immigrant tribes came the gods of the north and the repression of the deities of the southern peoples, a polarity which many scholars, notably Jane Ellen Harrison, characterize as the chthonian (Earth Mother) and the Olympian (Sky Father) religions.

Needless to say, Athene disappears from sight during this period, although her cult was clearly maintained, probably by surviving Mycenaeans who fled to regions not inundated by the new, primitive immigrants—among other places, to Athens, "the very city which had withstood the external upheavals" (Burkert 1985, 48). When she emerges to view again, it is the archaic age (ca. 750-480), when the Greeks had begun their climb back to the light of civilization. A new Greek language, based on the Phoenician alphabet, is created; populations are beginning to coalesce into city-states (the *polis*); trade routes are resumed and expanded; ideas are imported from more stable civilizations, in particular the Egyptian; laws and constitutions are laid in place; military forces are aggregated; and, true to Greek form, there is political shift after political shift and war after war, if not between city-states, with the Persians. And the Olympian pantheon is solidly in place.

Sometime early in this period, the literature of the Epic Cycle, all lost except for the *Iliad* and the *Odyssey*, is composed, the bard called Homer sings of the heroic Mycenaean past, and we get our first look at Athene under the patriarchy.

By Homer's time, Athene is no longer just the *potnia*, the house or palace guardian. Under the Mycenaean adaptations of the Minoan religion, she has already been revisioned: the Mycenaeans, almost always at war, took the mother goddess who guarded home and family and extended her responsibilities to the battlefield, where she was also to protect the king and his warriors. They did what every culture has done; they shaped their deities to meet their human needs. By the time the *Iliad* was composed, the official religion was no longer dominated by the goddess, and Athene's role as mother has been overshadowed by her function as battle maiden.

But here and there in the Homeric text we catch glimpses of Athene's older aspects. The text of the *Iliad* can, in fact, be read on one level as a revelation of the tensions between the old chthonian religion and the new Olympian one. Athene and Hera (along with Poseidon, also a chthonian deity of the Minoan-Mycenaean religion) are at loggerheads with Zeus, Apollo, and most of the rest of the Olympians, notably Ares. (An appropriate time to underscore that Ares, not Athene, was the true god of war; unlike Athene, whose primary interest is the protection of her people, Ares is brutal and bloodthirsty. Athene calls him "this maniacal god/by nature evil" [5, 548-9; Fitzgerald trans.].) Athene declares herself repeatedly to be a dutiful daughter of Zeus, but we begin to sense this to be self-protective rhetoric, since her actions continue to serve *her* purposes, not his. She knows how to escape his wrath, how to nod to authority without caving in to it, how to acknowledge the realities of power and politics and still follow the path she has determined for herself as the right one. Homer refers to her sullen anger against Zeus (4, 24-8); she has "waspish things to say, to irritate Zeus" (5, 481); in Book 8, 407-8, she calls Zeus evil and perverse, "full of a black madness." These are hardly the reactions and speeches of a Father's Daughter. Akhilleus speaks of a time when Athene, Hera, and Poseidon plotted to manacle Zeus and hold him in bondage (1, 457-68; all references are to the Fitzgerald translation). It is almost as though the chthonian Athene were rebelling against her forced subordination to the new, masculine order.

Throughout the epic the mothering defender predominates over the fierce battle maiden, and this balance is reflected in the epithets and appositions referring to Athene. Far more often than she is called by another other title she is simply "the grey-eyed goddess" (or a variant thereof). No doubt this is in part formulaic; in Greek, the phrase completes the Homeric dactylic hexameter line, and in any case it was one of the type of stock expressions which came to be attached to deities. But the repeated reference to grey eyes may also be a buried echo of an alternate birth myth in which Athene was the daughter of Poseidon. Akhilleus calls her "of the sea-grey eyes." Pausanias relates that Athene's image at the shrine of Hephaistos had grey eyes and noted that the Libyans "have written that Athene was the daughter of Poseidon and the Tritonian Lake and has Poseidon's grey-green eyes" (1, 44). The *Iliad* unwittingly connects Athene and Poseidon through color references. Scholars have noted that color is rarely used in Homeric literature, an infrequency which makes the appearance of color all the more significant. Of the 309 color references in the epic, 54 are to grey; of those, 34 are to Athene's eyes. Nearly all the rest are to the color of the sea, Poseidon's domain. Moreover, no one else's eyes are described by color, only Athene's. Such connectives may be made unconsciously, but they are never accidental or meaningless.

Next most frequently, she is called Pallas Athene, a title about which none of the scholars can seem to agree. "Pallas" may mean simply "maiden," as Harrison asserts, or it may be a reference to her friend, Pallas, whose name Athene added to her own; or it may allude to yet another birth myth in which Athene was said to be the daughter neither of Zeus nor of Poseidon but of a giant named Pallas.

Homer's text also refers to her as Daughter of Zeus, dazzling, formidable, defender, guardian, first on Olympos, goddess of goddesses, and, with some frequency, Hope of Soldiers. But only once is she linked with war (by Diomedes, when he calls her "divine mistress of war"), and the only personage who calls her a "destroyer" with a "violent heart" is the testy Ares, whose reliability as an objective observer is thrown into question by the fact that he also calls her a "dogfly." Clearly, it was her role as motherly and fierce guardian which predominated over whatever appetite she may have been thought to have for war.

One of the things we observe about Athene as she moves in the epics from one context to another is that she was an accomplished shape-shifter. In the *Iliad* she appears only twice in human guise, as Laodokos to Pandoros, and as Deiphobos to Hektor—both, appropriately enough in the context, soldiers speaking to soldiers. That is, she took the form which would produce the desired effect and which suited the context. Always the consummate pragmatist, Athene is still sensitive to the nuances of relationships, but she is never sentimental. In the *Odyssey* she takes on many more human forms than she does in the *Iliad* because there is more variety in circumstances and in the cast of characters. It would seem that she has a fine grasp of psychology, or at least of human nature, for without fail she understands the needs of the individual and in what form that individual will best hear what he or she needs to hear. So Athene appears as an old family friend and father figure to the young Telemachos; as sister to Penelopeia; as a peer to Nausikaa; as a young shepherd to guide Odysseus in the mists veiling Ithake upon his return. Interestingly, where in the *Iliad* it is the color of her eyes that is most mentioned, in the *Odyssey* it is their bright and flashing aspect, as though to call attention to the clarity of vision that is needed as she moves from one set of circumstances to another. This aspect of Athene's look has often been translated as "glinting," "flashing," or "fierce," and may very well have been yet another association of the goddess with the snake. Bruno Snell's comments in this regard are worth quoting at length:

> Homer uses a great variety of verbs to denote the operation of sight. . . . Of these, several have gone out of use in later Greek. . . . Only two words make their appearance after the time of Homer. . . . The words which were discarded tell us that the older language recognized certain needs which were no longer felt by its successor. δερκεσθαι means: to have a particular look in one's eyes. δρακων, the snake, whose name is derived from δερκεσθαι, owes this designation to the uncanny glint in his eye. He is called "the seeing one", not because he can see particularly well, but because his stare commands attention. By the same token Homer's δερκεσθαι refers not so much to the function of the eye as to its gleam as noticed by someone else. The verb is used of the Gorgon whose glance incites terror, and of the raging boar whose eyes radiate fire. . . . It denotes an "expressive signal" or "gesture" of the eyes. . . . The verbs of the early period, it appears, take their cue from the palpable aspects, the external qualifications, of the act of seeing, while later on it is the essential function itself, the operation common to every glance, which determines the content of the verb. . . . It goes without saying that even in Homer men used their eyes "to see", i.e., to receive optical impressions. But apparently they took no decisive interest in what we justly regard as the basic function, the objective essence, of sight; and if they had no word for it, it follows that as far as they were concerned it did not exist. (Snell 1953, 2-5)

It would appear, then, that the qualities of brightness, clarity, and fierceness which in our diction are efforts to describe at least in part the experience of the *one who sees* were in Homer's time descriptions of what the *person being looked at saw*. This suggests that by the time of Homer, the populace desperately needed a deity who possessed extraordinary capacities for clear vision. That would not be surprising, given the sometime disarray of the archaic age and the often erratic behaviors ascribed to the rest of the Olympian pantheon.

Whatever the intricacies of archaic Greek, we can be sure that by Homer's day Athene was well on her way to being the goddess of Wisdom and Reason, among her primary attributes by the time of the classical age. The same bright look which connects her with the chthonic snake, the Gorgon, and the mother religion in the Minoan-Mycenaean culture becomes the look of the fiercely guarding mother in the late Mycenaean, and then, in Attica in the classical age, the symbol of clarity of intellect. Sokrates, in Plato's "Cratylus," is quite explicit about this, although he ascribes the explanation to an earlier time:

> For most of these [ancients] in their explanations of the poet [Homer], assert that he meant by Athene "mind" . . . and "intelligence" . . . and the maker of names appears to have had a singular notion about her; and indeed calls her by a still higher title, "divine intelligence" . . . as though he would say: this is she who has the mind of god. . . . Nor shall we be far wrong in supposing that the author of it wished to identify this goddess with moral intelligence. . . . (1952, 407; Jowett trans.)

This kind of thinking about Athene, along with the story of her birth from the forehead of Zeus and other mythologems, caused Harrison to argue that it was the Athenians who would "lift her from all earthly contact. . . . It is this that lends to the figure of Athena an aloofness, that makes of her, for all her beauty, something of an abstraction, an unreality; she is Reason, Light and Liberty . . . " (1963, 73-4). Elsewhere she writes:

> The rising democracy not unnaturally revived the ancient figure of the Kore, but in reviving her they strangely altered her being and reft from her much of her beauty and reality. They made her a sexless

thing, neither man nor woman. . . . Nowhere is this artificiality, this unreality of Athene . . . so keenly felt as in the famous myth of her birth from the brain of Zeus. A poet may see its splendour . . . but it remains a desperate theological expedient to rid an earth-born Kore of her matriarchal conditions. (1991, 302)

Harrison notwithstanding, it is plausible to argue that the Athenians, rather than "reviving" the goddess, were instead the prime force in keeping alive her cult after the demise of the Mycenaean civilization. The region of Attica, of which Athens became the foremost city, had been as Mycenaean as any— the Akropolis was first a Mycenaean royal-religious site. Even the name "Athenai" is not a Greek word and may represent the evolution of a Minoan place-name. And, of course, Homer mentioned Athens in the Catalogue of Ships, the long list of Mycenaean cities which gathered forces to fight in the Trojan War; the Catalogue itself is thought to be a piece of history origi- nated in Mycenaean times and passed down over the centuries from bard to bard. Moreover, Athens, as we have seen, was among the few places virtu- ally untouched by the forces which decimated the Argive and other regions, and was in a position to provide continuity with the older order—specially in view of the fact that many Mycenaeans fled to Athens.

It should not be construed from this, however, that Athens leapt into prominence with the demise of the old order. Not until the late Dark Age/ early archaic did city-states begin to coalesce, and it was not until 480, after the Persian Wars, that Athens became the Greek supernova. Until the classical period, whose reputation belies its brief life of little more than a century, cultural supremacy shifted from Ionia to Athens to Corinth, and political supremacy was even less secure: power resided in the Euboean cities of Chalcis and Eretria, then Corinth, then Sparta, and finally, but briefly, in Athens. As Athens became stronger and eventually the center of a more-or-less unified Attica, it came to embody what to our perspective may seem opposing inter- ests: on the one hand, it was almost constantly engaged in warfare, the prevailing tenor of relations among the various Greek regions being one of unabashed hostility; on the other hand, Athens became the great cultural center where the activity of the creative intellect was supremely valued. For these reasons, it is possible to argue that Athens carried the tradition of the *potnia*, altering her attributes and imagery over time to reflect what it valued most, the life of the mind, but retaining her function as battle maiden.

Perhaps for this reason, then, the goddess who had been simply "Lady" lost all other primary identifications with place and settled into her final and exclusive identifications with the city-state of Athens. This evolution may explain why Homer, composing as he did sometime between 750 and 650, tells in the *Iliad* that when Athene returned to the Akropolis it was not to her own temple but to one she shared with Erichthonios. The Akropolis did not become the cult center of Athene Polias until the sixth century.

Scholars have argued, without agreeing on an answer, the question of whether Athens took its name from the goddess or the goddess her name from the city. Burkert describes this as "an ancient dispute," and adds, "Since -*ene* is a typical place-name suffix . . . the goddess most probably takes her name from the city" (1985, 139). This, however, is in direct conflict with Nilsson, who concluded that Athens took its name from Athene. "It is of course impossible to decide whether this name originally belonged exclusively to Athens or was commoner and more wide-spread." There were, he points out, other towns with the same name, in Euboea and in Boiotia. "In the historical age it is, however, evident that Athena ousted many other city-goddesses and appropriated their names as secondary names, e.g., Alea and Itonia, and gradually developed into a common protectress of the towns" (1949, 490). Nilsson also observes that the suffix -*ene* is Mycenaean, not Greek.

It seems that there are a number of reasons to agree with the earlier scholar. Athene in all likelihood was already part of the Mycenaean pantheon by the time of the Late Bronze Age, the date of the Linear B tablets. Since deities do not spring up overnight, we may assume that Athene was, by whatever name, long established as a distinct person before then. It would not be unreasonable to think that she was recognized, probably still as the Minoized house guardian, during the early Bronze Age, certainly by the later centuries of that period, 3000 to 2000. Now it happens that during that millenium Athens, on the archaeological evidence, was virtually abandoned, probably because it was too far from the sea to participate in the vigorous maritime activity of the era. The city began to show some signs of life during the Middle Bronze Age (2000-1600), but did not flourish until the Late Bronze Age (1600-1100) (Camp 1986, 25). If it is a correct conjecture that the goddess was in place in the Minoan-Mycenaean pantheon by the final centuries of the Early Bronze Age, it can be argued that she would not have taken her name from an abandoned city of no consequence.

It is far more likely that the city, once it became viable again, would claim the name and protection of an already venerated and puissant goddess.

But Karl Kerényi probably puts forth the simplest and most persuasive argument. Writing of her title "Athene, the Guardian of Athens" (*Athena e Athenon medeousa*), he makes this wonderfully clear observation:

> The old question . . . must be adjudicated in favor of the first alternative (the town was named after the goddess): if "Athene" had originally signified merely the "goddess of the town of fortress Athens," there would have been no need to refer to her as "Athene of Athens." (1978, 28)

In the final analysis, unless there are further discoveries of records such as the Pylian tablets and/or the decipherment of the Linear A tablets from Knossos, which promise to reveal more about religion, the naming of Athene will probably remain a tantalizing and in the end insoluble puzzle.

Even the classical period does not quite forget that Athene's origins were not Olympian. In the "Hymn to Athena," the brevity of which argues its composition during the classical age, we are presented again with Zeus' parentage but also with Athene's epithet "Tritogene" (usually "Tritogeneia"), a title which also appears in the *Iliad* and, as mentioned above, connects her with her autochthonous birth. Pindar refers to her birth from Zeus' head (Olympia 7) but also to her sacred wood (Olympia 5), which can be seen as a remnant of the Minoan-Mycenaean tree cult. In Pythia 12, he recounts Athene's invention of the flute, which she bestows on mortals for their use. The Homeric Hymns reiterate the usual birth myth and Athene's "love of war" but also her role as inventor, bronzesmith, and creator of the decorative arts (hymns to Aphrodite and to Hephaistos).

The old chthonian order was, in fact, never completely abandoned. Howe (1954) points out that on the west pediment of the early sixth century temple of Artemis at Corcyra, "three distinctly different themes were represented . . . which symbolized the triad of beliefs that absorbed Greeks of that period: the literary interest, represented by the Homeric figure of Priam slain by Neoptolemos; the Olympian religion, represented by a tiny Zeus slaying a giant; and superstitious belief, in the Gorgon and flanking animals. From the outstanding size and station of the Gorgon it is obvious that the demonic element predominated" (215).

Bibliography

Aischylos (Aeschylus). 1953. *Oresteia*. Translated by Richard Lattimore. Chicago: Univ. of Chicago Press.

Aristotle. 1952. *Nichomachean Ethics*. Translated by W. D. Ross; *Politics*. Translated by Benjamin Jowett. Chicago: Encyclopaedia Britannica, Inc.

Armstrong, A. Hilary. 1987. "The Divine Enhancement of Earthly Beauties: The Hellenic and Platonic Tradition." *The Eranos Lecture Series*. Dallas: Spring Publications, Inc.

Arrowsmith, William. 1969. Introduction to *Aristophanes: Three Comedies*. Ann Arbor: Univ. of Michigan Press.

Auden, W. H. 1958. "Reflections upon reading Werner Jaeger's *Paideia*." *The Griffin* (March 1958), Reader's Subscription, Inc.

Benedict, Ruth. 1989. *The Chrysanthemum and the Sword*. Boston: Houghton Mifflin Co. (First published in 1946.)

Bergson, Henri. 1954. *The Two Sources of Morality and Religion*. Garden City, NY: Doubleday & Co. (First published in 1932.)

Boer, Charles. 1970. Introduction to *The Homeric Hymns*. Translated by Charles Boer. Dallas: Spring Publications, Inc..

Burkert, Walter. 1985. *Greek Religion*. (No loc.): Basil Blackwell.

Camp, John M. 1986. *The Athenian Agora*. London: Thames and Hudson Ltd.

Carotenuto, Aldo. 1989. *Eros and Pathos*. Toronto: Inner City Books.

_____. 1992. *The Difficult Art: A Critical Discourse on Psychotherapy*. Translated by Joan Tambureno. Wilmette, IL: Chiron Publications.

Chadwick, John. 1963. *The Decipherment of Linear B*. New York: Vintage Books.

Coss, Richard G. 1992. "Reflections on the Evil Eye." In *The Evil Eye*, edited by Alan Dundes. Madison, WI: The Univ. of Wisconsin Press. (First published in 1981.)

Devambez, Pierre. 1962. *Greek Painting*. New York: The Viking Press.

Dodds, E. R. 1951. *The Greeks and the Irrational*. Berkeley: Univ. of California Press.

Douglas, Mary. 1970. *Purity and Danger*. Baltimore: Penguin Books. (First published in 1966.)

Edinger, Edward F. 1974. *Ego and Archetype*. Baltimore: Penguin Books.

_____. 1984. *The Creation of Consciousness*. Toronto: Inner City Books.

Eliade, Mircea. 1959. *The Sacred and the Profane*. Translated by Willard R. Trask. New York: Harcourt, Brace and World, Inc.

_____. 1960. *Myths, Dreams and Mysteries*. Translated by Philip Mairet. New York: Harper Brothers.

Engelsman, Joan Chamberlain. 1987. *The Feminine Dimension of the Divine*. Wilmette, IL: Chiron Books.

Feldman, Thalia. 1965. "Gorgo and the Origins of Fear." *Arion* 4: 484-494.

Finley, M. I. 1979. *The World of Odysseus*. New York: Penguin Books.

Fordham, Michael. 1962. "The Theory of Archetypes as Applied to Child Development with Particular Reference to the Self." In *The Archetype*, Proceedings of the 2nd International Congress of Analytical Psychologists, 48-62. Basel/New York: S. Karger.

_____. 1985. "Abandonment in Infancy." In *Chiron: A Review of Jungian Analysis*, edited by Nathan Schwartz-Salant and Murray Stein. 1-21. Wilmette, IL: Chiron Books.

Forrest, George. 1989. "Greece: The History of the Archaic Period." In *Greece and the Hellenistic World*. Edited by John Boardman, Jasper Griffin, and Oswyn Murray. Oxford/New York: Oxford Univ. Press.

Freud, Sigmund. n.d. [1927]. *The Future of an Illusion*. Translated by W. D. Robson-Scott. Garden City, NY: Doubleday and Co.

Georgiades, Thrasybulos. n.d. *Greek Music, Verse and Dance*. New York: Merlin Press.

Graves, Robert. 1948. *The White Goddess*. No loc.: Farrar Straus and Cudahy.

——————. 1959. *The Greek Myths*. New York: George Braziller, Inc.

Guntrip, Harry. 1973. *Psychoanalytic Theory, Therapy, and the Self*. New York: Basic Books.

Hadas, Moses. 1960. *The Greek Ideal and its Survival*. New York: Harper and Row.

Harding, Esther. 1965. *The Parental Image*. New York: G. P. Putnam's and Sons.

——————. 1971. *Woman's Mysteries*. New York: Harper and Row.

Harrison, Jane Ellen. 1918. *Ancient Art and Ritual*. London: Thornton Butterworth Ltd.

——————. 1963. *Mythology*. New York: Harcourt, Brace and World, Inc. (First published in 1924.)

——————. 1991. *Prolegomena to the Study of Greek Religion*. Princeton, NJ: Princeton Univ. Press (Mythos Series). (First published in 1903.)

Henderson, Joseph L. and Maud V. Oakes. 1991. *The Wisdom of the Serpent*. New York: George Braziller, Inc. (First published in 1963.)

Herman, Nini. 1988. *My Kleinian Home*. London: Free Association Books.

——————. 1989. *Too Long a Child: The Mother-Daughter Dyad*. London: Free Association Books.

Hesiod. 1959. *Hesiod: The Homeric Hymns and Homerica*. Translated by H. G. Evelyn-White. Cambridge: Harvard Univ. Press (Loeb Library).

——. 1973. *Hesiod and Theognis*. Translated by Dorothea Wender. Harmondsworth, Middlesex, England: Penguin Books.

Hillman, James. 1967. *Insearch: Psychology and Religion*. New York: Charles Scribner's Sons.

——————. 1975. *Re-visioning Psychology*. New York: Harper and Row.

——————. 1979. "An Essay on Pan." In *Pan and the Nightmare*. Irving, TX: Spring Publications, Inc.

——————. 1980. "On the Necessity of Abnormal Psychology: Ananke and Athene." In *Facing the Gods*. Edited by James Hillman. Dallas, TX: Spring Publications, Inc.

Homer. 1937. *The Odyssey*. Translated by W. H. D. Rouse. New York: New American Library.

_____. 1989. *The Iliad*. Translated by Robert Fitzgerald. New York: Doubleday and Company.

_____. 1990. *The Iliad*. Translated by Robert Fagles. New York: Viking Press.

Hopkins, Adam. 1977. *Crete: Its Past, Present and People*. London: Faber and Faber.

Howe, Thalia Phillies. 1954. "The Origin and Function of the Gorgon-head." In *American Journal of Archaeology*. 58, 3:209-221.

_____. 1969. "The Primitive Presence in Pre-classical Greece." In *Primitive Views of the World*. Edited by Stanley Diamond. New York: Columbia Univ. Press.

Hultberg, Peer. 1988. "Shame—A Hidden Emotion." In *Journal of Analytical Psychology*. 33:109-126.

Jaeger, Werner. 1945. *Paideia: the Ideals of Greek Culture*. Translated by Gilbert Highet. 3 vols. New York: Oxford Univ. Press.

Jung, Carl Gustav. 1959. *Aion: Researches into the Phenomenology of the Self*. Translated by R. F. C. Hull. Princeton: Princeton Univ. Press (Bollingen Series XX).

_____. 1961. *Memories, Dreams, and Reflections*. Translated by Richard and Clara Winston. New York: Random House.

_____. 1962. Foreword and commentary to *The Secret of the Golden Flower*. Translated by Cary F. Baynes. New York: Harcourt, Brace and World, Inc.

_____. 1963. *Mysterium Coniunctionis*. Translated by R. F. C. Hull. Princeton: Princeton Univ. Press.

_____. 1966a. *The Psychology of the Transference*. Translated by R. F. C. Hull. Princeton: Princeton Univ. Press (Bollingen Series XX). (First published in 1954.)

_____. 1966b. "Introduction to Frances Wickes." in *The Inner World of Childhood*. Englewood Cliffs, NJ: Prentice-Hall. (First published in 1927.)

_____. 1967. *Symbols of Transformation*. Translated by R. F. C. Hull. Princeton: Princeton Univ. Press (Bollingen Series XX). (First published in 1956.)

_____. 1969. *Essays on a Science of Mythology* (with C. Kerényi). Translated by R. F. C. Hull. Princeton: Princeton Univ. Press (Bollingen Series XXII). (First published in 1949.)

_____. 1973. *C. G. Jung Letters*. Translated by R. F. C. Hull. 2 vols. Princeton: Princeton Univ. Press (Bollingen Series XCV.)

_____. 1976. *Psychological Types*. Translated by H. G. Baynes. Princeton: Princeton Univ. Press (Bollingen Series XX). (First published in 1971.)

Kaufman, Gershen. 1989. *The Psychology of Shame*. New York: Springer Publishing Company.

Kerényi, Carl. 1951. *The Gods of the Greeks*. (No loc.): Thames and Hudson.

_____. 1978. *Athene, Virgin and Mother in Greek Religion*. Dallas: Spring Publications, Inc.

Kirk, G. S. 1975. *The Nature of Greek Myths*. Woodstock, NY: The Overlook Press.

Kitto, H. D. F. 1960. *The Greeks*. Baltimore: Penguin Books.

Knox, Bernard. 1990. Introduction and notes to *The Iliad*. Translated by Robert Fagles. New York: Viking Press.

Kohut, Heinz. 1977. *The Restoration of the Self*. New York: International Universities Press, Inc.

Levi, Peter. 1971. Introduction and notes to *Pausanias: Guide to Greece*. 2 vols. London: Penguin Books.

Lewis, C. S. 1962. *They Asked for a Paper*. London: Geoffrey Bles.

Luke, Helen M. 1987. *Old Age*. New York: Parabola Books.

Lynd, Helen Merrell. 1958. *On Shame and the Search for Identity*. New York: Harcourt, Brace and World, Inc.

Mahler, Margaret S. 1968. *On Human Symbiosis and the Vicissitudes of Individuation*. New York: International Universities Press.

Merton, Thomas. 1972. *New Seeds of Contemplation*. New York: New Directions. (First published in 1962.)

Miller, Alice. 1981. *Prisoners of Childhood*. Translated by Ruth Ward. New York: Basic Books.

_____. 1984. *Thou Shalt not be Aware: Society's Betrayal of the Child*. Translated by Hildegarde and Hunter Hannum. New York: Farrar, Straus & Giroux.

Miller, David L. 1981. *The New Polytheism*. Dallas: Spring Publications, Inc.

Morrison, Andrew P. 1989. *Shame: the Underside of Narcissism*. Hillsdale, NJ: The Analytic Press.

Murray, Gilbert. 1955. *Five Stages of Greek Religion*. Garden City, NY: Doubleday and Company.

Murray, Oswyn. 1989. "Life and Society in Classical Greece." In *Greece and the Hellenistic World*. Edited by John Boardman, Jasper Griffin, and Oswyn Murray. Oxford/New York: Oxford Univ. Press.

Napier, A. David. 1986. *Masks, Transformation, and Paradox*. Berkeley, CA: Univ. of California Press.

Nathanson, Donald L. 1992. *Shame and Pride: Affect, Sex, and the Birth of the Self*. New York: W. W. Norton and Company.

Neumann, Erich. 1963. *The Great Mother*. Translated by Ralph Manheim. Princeton: Princeton Univ. Press (Bollingen Series XLVII). (First published in 1955.)

_____. 1970. *The Origins and History of Consciousness*. Translated by R. F. C. Hull. Princeton: Princeton Univ. Press (Bollingen Series XLII). (First published in 1949.)

_____. 1990. *The Child: Structure and Dynamics of the Nascent Personality*. Translated by Ralph Manheim. Boston: Shambhala. (First published in 1973.)

Nietzsche, Friedrich. 1910. *Human, All-too-Human*. Translated by Helen Zimmern. Part I, *The Complete Works of Friedrich Nietzsche*, vol. 6, edited by Oscar Levy. London: T. N. Foulis.

_____. 1911. *Human, All-too-Human*. Translated by Paul V. Cohn. Part II, *The Complete Works of Friedrich Nietzsche*, vol. 7, edited by Oscar Levy. London: T. N. Foulis.

Nilsson, Martin Persson. 1949. *Minoan-Mycenaean Religion and its Survival in Greek Religion*. London: Oxford Univ. Press. (First published in 1927.)

Nussbaum, Martha Craven. 1980. "Shame, Separateness, and Political Unity: Aristotle's Criticism of Plato." In *Essays on Aristotle's Ethics*. Edited by Amélie Oksenberg Rorty. Berkeley, CA: Univ. of California Press.

Ogden, Thomas H. 1988. "Misrecognitions and the Fear of Not Knowing," in *The Psychoanalytic Quarterly* 57: 643-666.

Otto, Rudolf. 1958. *The Idea of the Holy: An Inquiry into the Non-rational Factor in the Idea of the Divine and its Relation to the Rational*. Translated by John W. Harvey. New York: Oxford Univ. Press. (First published in 1923.)

Parker, Robert. 1989. "Greek Religion." In *Greece and the Hellenistic World*. Edited by John Boardman, Jasper Griffin, and Oswyn Murray. Oxford/New York: Oxford Univ. Press.

Pausanias. 1971. *Guide to Greece*. 2 vols. Translated with an introduction by Peter Levi. London: Penguin Books.

Perera, Sylvia Brinton. 1986. *The Scapegoat Complex*. Toronto: Inner City Books.

Piers, G. and M. B. Singer. 1953. *Shame and Guilt*. New York: W. W. Norton and Company.

Pindar. 1947. *Odes*. Translated by Richard Lattimore. Chicago: Univ. of Chicago Press.

Plato. 1952. *The Dialogues of Plato*. Translated by Benjamin Jowett. Chicago: Encyclopaedia Brittanica, Inc.

Pruyser, Paul W. 1968. *A Dynamic Psychology of Religion*. New York: Harper and Row.

Restak, Richard M. 1986. *The Infant Mind*. Garden City, NY: Doubleday and Company.

Ricoeur, Paul. 1967. *The Symbolism of Evil*. Translated by Emerson Buchanan. Boston: Beacon Press.

_____. 1986. *Fallible Man*. Translated by Charles A. Kelbley. New York: Fordham Univ. Press. (First published 1960.)

Rose, H. J. 1968. *Gods and Heroes of the Greeks*. Cleveland and New York: World Publishing Co.

_____. 1991. *A Handbook of Greek Mythology*. New York: Penguin Books.

Sanford, John A. 1981. *Evil: The Shadow Side of Reality*. New York: Crossroad Press.

Sarton, May. 1978. *Selected Poems*. New York: W. W. Norton and Company, Inc.

Sartre, Jean-Paul. 1955. *Being and Nothingness: An Essay on Phenomenological Ontology*. Translated by Hazel E. Barnes. New York: The Philosophical Library.

Schneider, Carl D. 1992. *Shame: Exposure and Privacy*. New York: W. W. Norton and Company, Inc.

Sidoli, Mara. 1988. "Shame and the Shadow." In *The Journal of Analytical Psychology* 33:127-142.

Snell, Bruno. 1953. *The Discovery of the Mind*. Translated by T. G. Rosenmeyer. Cambridge, MA: Harvard Univ. Press.

Sophocles. 1969. *The Oedipus Cycle*. Translated by Dudley Fitts and Robert Fitzgerald. New York: Harcourt, Brace and World, Inc.

Stein, Robert. 1973. *Incest and Human Love*. Dallas: Spring Publications, Inc.

Ulanov, Ann Belford. 1987. "The God You Touch." In Parabola 12, 3:18-33.

Van Nortwick, Thomas. 1992. *Somewhere I Have Never Travelled: The Second Self and the Hero's Journey in Ancient Epic*. Oxford/New York: Oxford Univ. Press.

Vermeule, Emily. 1972. *Greece in the Bronze Age*. Chicago: Univ. of Chicago Press. (First published in 1964.)

Vernant, Jean-Pierre. 1990. *Myth and Society in Ancient Greece*. Translated by Janet Lloyd. New York: Zone Books.

Von Franz, Marie-Louise. 1981. *Puer Aeternus*. Santa Monica, CA: Sigo Press. (First published in 1970.)

_____. 1983. *Shadow and Evil in Fairytales*. Dallas: Spring Publications, Inc. (First published in 1974.)

_____. 1993. *Psychotherapy*. Boston and London: Shambhala.

Williams, Bernard. 1993. *Shame and Necessity*. Berkeley, CA: Univ. of California Press.

Winnicott, D. W. 1975. *Through Paediatrics to Psycho-Analysis*. New York: Basic Books.

_____. 1988. *Human Nature*. New York: Schocken Books.

Wittgenstein, Ludwig. 1961. *Tractatus Logico-Philosophicus*. London: Routledge and Kegan Paul.

Wood, Michael. 1985. *In Search of the Trojan War*. New York: New American Library.

Woodward, Jocelyn M. 1937. *Perseus: A Study in Greek Art and Legend*. Cambridge: Cambridge Univ. Press.

Wurmser, Léon. 1995. *The Mask of Shame*. Northvale, NJ: Jason Aronson, Inc. (First published in 1981.)

Zeller, Max. 1990. *The Dream: The Vision of the Night*. Boston: Sigo Press. (First published in 1975.)

About the Author

Sandra Prewitt Edelman holds advanced degrees in counselling psychology and in literature. A former educator and prize-winning poet, she has written for theatre and film as well as in the fields of anthropology (most notably for the *Smithsonian Handbook of North American Indians*) and literary criticism. Her fiction, essays, and poetry have appeared in *The Southwest Review* and *Carolina Quarterly,* among others, and she has served as editor for several literary magazines. Works in progress are a novel and a revisionist study of the Eros figure. Her home is in Santa Fe, New Mexico.

Other Pagan Works Published by Spring

Athene: Virgin and Mother in Greek Religion
KARL KERÉNYI
The awesome goddess who affects the fates of both women and men, Athene unites the virginal father's daughter and the encouraging mother of the spirit. Kerényi's careful rendering of the many aspects of her mythos demonstrares a profound understanding of feminine intelligence both in its fierceness and its darker animal nature—especially apparent in the symbolism of the owl, goat, horse, and Gorgon. The archetypal image of Athene provides a background of communal and political consciousness, individuality, and the power of mind. (125 pp.)

The Homeric Hymns
CHARLES BOER, TR.
This translation, nominated for the National Book Award, has established itself like nothing else. The 2000 year old book gives the earliest depiction of the divinities as individuals and evokes the Greek mythic imagination. William Arrowsmith writes, "[though] there were translations in plenty, there was nothing like this remarkable work in which Greek gods appear not as abstract presences but as moving and radiant irruptions of the sacred." (182 pp.)

Catullus's Complete Poetic Works
JACOB RABINOWITZ, TR.
This bold, yet literal translation grasps the elegance, passion and nastiness not only of the ancient Roman poet but also of first-century B.C. Rome. William S. Burroughs says of this work, "Beautifully translated . . . trivial, frivolous, profound, obscene. Hear the fossils of lust." Underground writer Thom Metzger affirms, "It's more fun than waving a dog's head on a stick at your mother." (150 pp.)

Spring Publications, Inc. • 299 East Quassett Road
Woodstock, Connecticut 06281
tel. (860) 974-3428
http://www.neca.com/~spring